IMAGES
of America

BARNEGAT
LIFE BY THE BAY

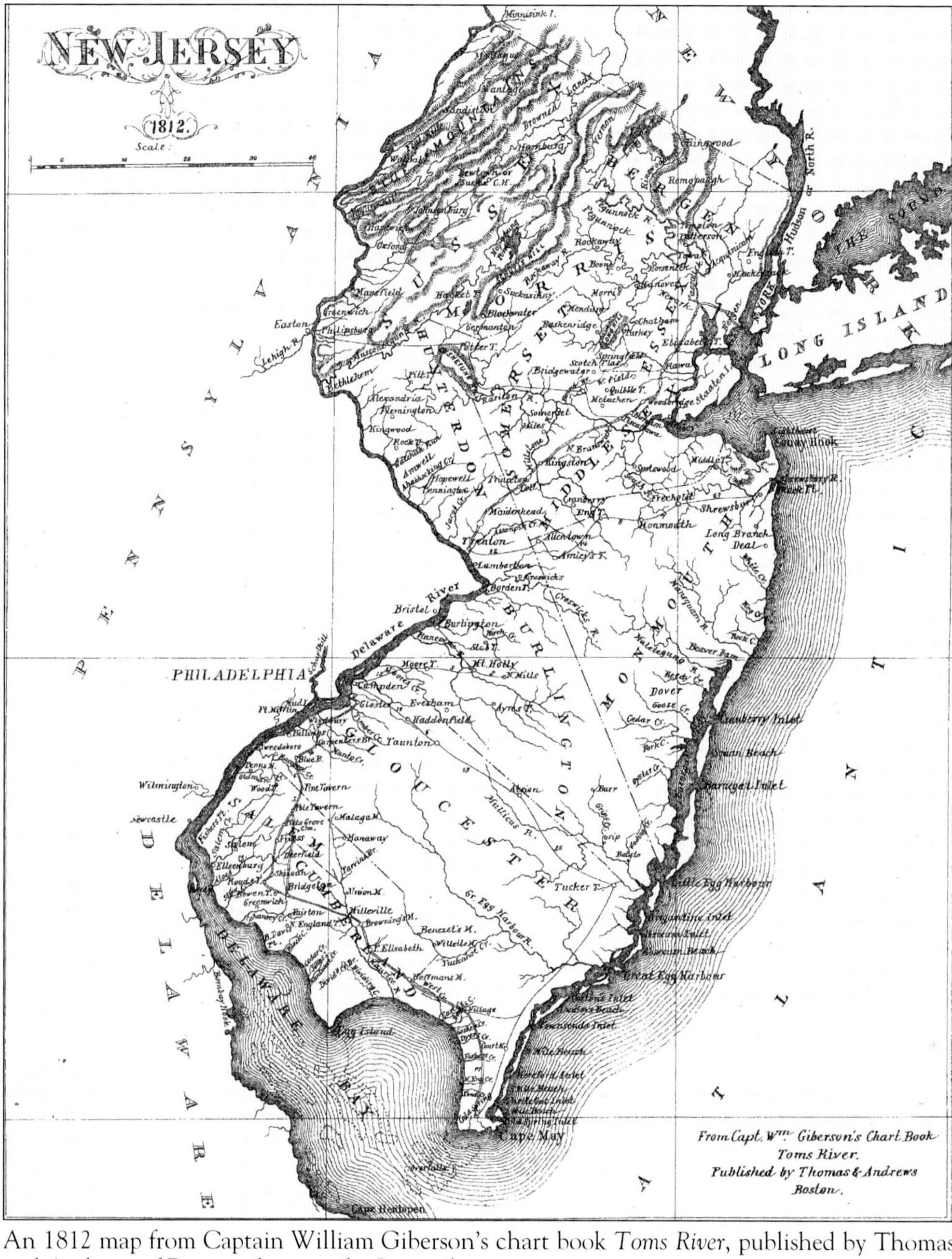

An 1812 map from Captain William Giberson's chart book *Toms River*, published by Thomas and Andrews of Boston, showing the Jersey shore.

IMAGES
of America

BARNEGAT
LIFE BY THE BAY

Kevin Hughes

ARCADIA
PUBLISHING

ISBN 978-0-7385-8971-8

Published by Arcadia Publishing
Charleston, South Carolina

Printed in the United States of America

For all general information contact Arcadia Publishing at:
Telephone 843-853-2070
Fax 843-853-0044
E-mail sales@arcadiapublishing.com
For customer service and orders:
Toll-Free 1-888-313-2665

Visit us on the Internet at www.arcadiapublishing.com

Contents

Acknowledgments

This endeavor to portray the life and times of the people of Barnegat and the Barnegat Bay area through photographs could not have been possible without the help and support of my wife, Kathy, and my son Evan. Their assistance, support, patience, and tolerance helped me to assemble my personal collection of historic photographs shown here. Many miles and hours were spent collecting and researching these old vintage images. It is through these photographs, some seen here for the very first time, that we can see how the area has grown and changed through the last one hundred or so years.

Thanks go to Frederick Watts, a fellow collector and historian who contributed several photographs to help complete this book, and also to the Barnegat Historical Society for photographs and important background information on Barnegat's great ship captains.

Introduction

Barnegat, which derives its name from the Dutch words "Barning Gat," means "breakers inlet." It was named by the Dutch navigator Captain Mey, after whom the shore town of Cape May was named. It was first charted by the famous explorer Henry Hudson in his ship's log entry dated September 2, 1609. Here he described a "great lake of water," which was actually the Barnegat Bay. The "mouth of the lake," as he described it, is known today as the Barnegat Inlet.

The original inhabitants of Barnegat were actually our very first "tourists." Long before the Dutch visited the area, tribes of New Jersey Indians were known to have taken seasonal treks here from their Central Jersey homes. The summer was the time to take advantage of the great fishing and clamming opportunities of the area. Once a sufficient supply of food for the winter was acquired, they would return inland to their winter homes. The first white settlers would not arrive here until 1720, when the first home in Barnegat was built. Some of the first settlers bear very familiar names to those in the area today: Ridgway, Birdsall, Cranmer, and Collins.

The first church in Barnegat was built in 1767 by the Quakers. Many early settlers practiced the strict Quaker religion, which explains the lack of Barnegat's participation in both the Revolutionary and Civil Wars, as they were opposed to fighting and violence. Instead, Barnegat's residents would turn to the sea for their livelihood. As early as the Revolutionary War period, Barnegat's men were plying the sea in locally built tall-masted ships. They sailed near and far transporting cedar, pine, and charcoal to worldwide ports. Stories of far-away places, great storms, and pirates were commonplace. Ship- and boat-building as well as the role of the seaman would remain a very active part of Barnegat's economy until the advent of the railroads and the steamboats in the 1870s.

Barnegat's history reads like a great adventure novel. It is sprinkled with stories of great sailing ships, steam locomotives, and pirates. Odd industries like silkworm-raising, mink-farming, and glassblowing are long gone. And also gone are the days of ice delivery, collecting moss, and the building of thousands of sneakbox boats. Within these pages are the fascinating people of Barnegat's past, seen through the lens of a camera. This book is a tribute to all of them, as well as a valuable history lesson to today's children—Barnegat's future.

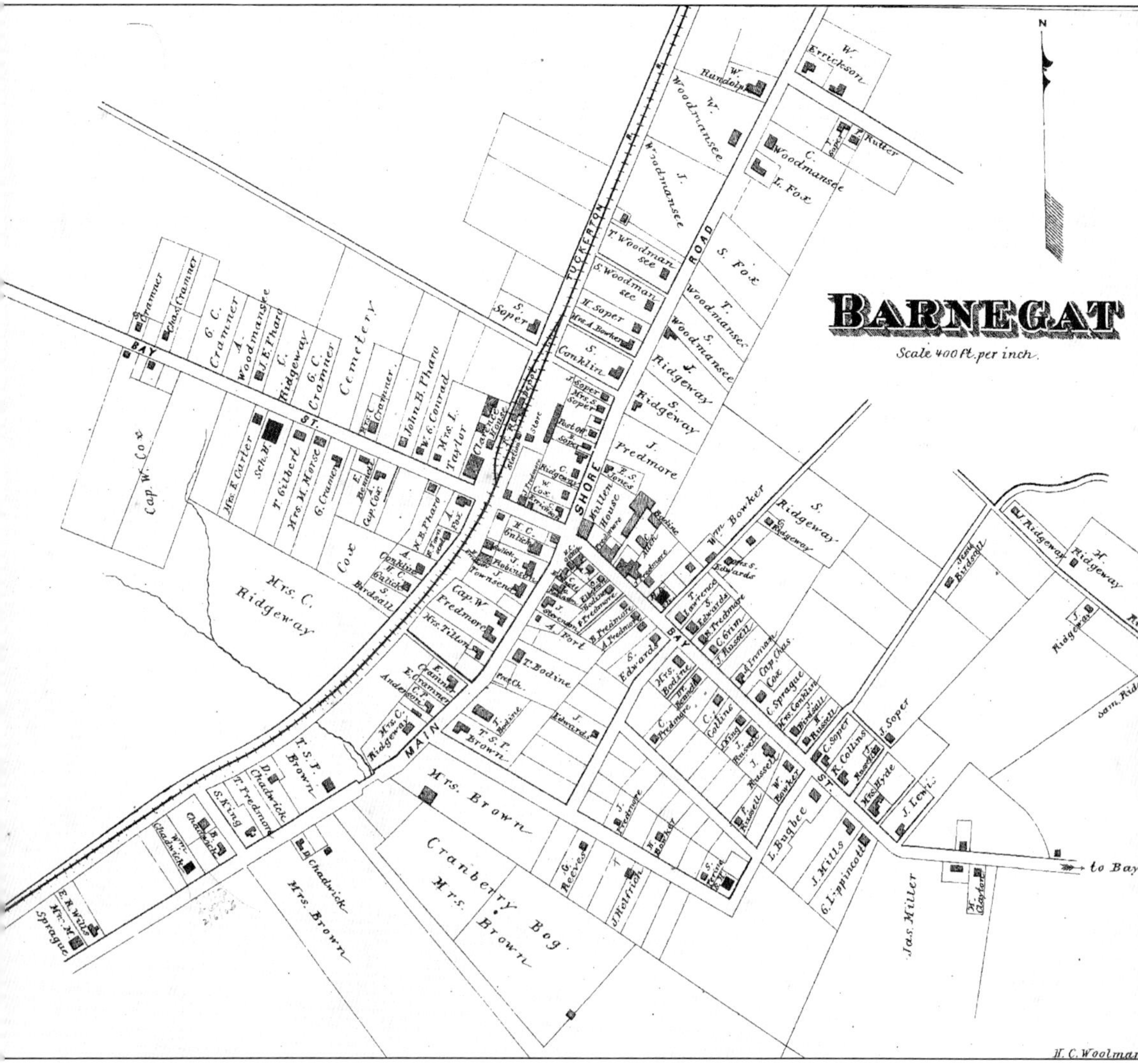

The village of Barnegat as it appeared in the 1878 Woolman and Rose atlas of the New Jersey coast.

One

Life Around Town

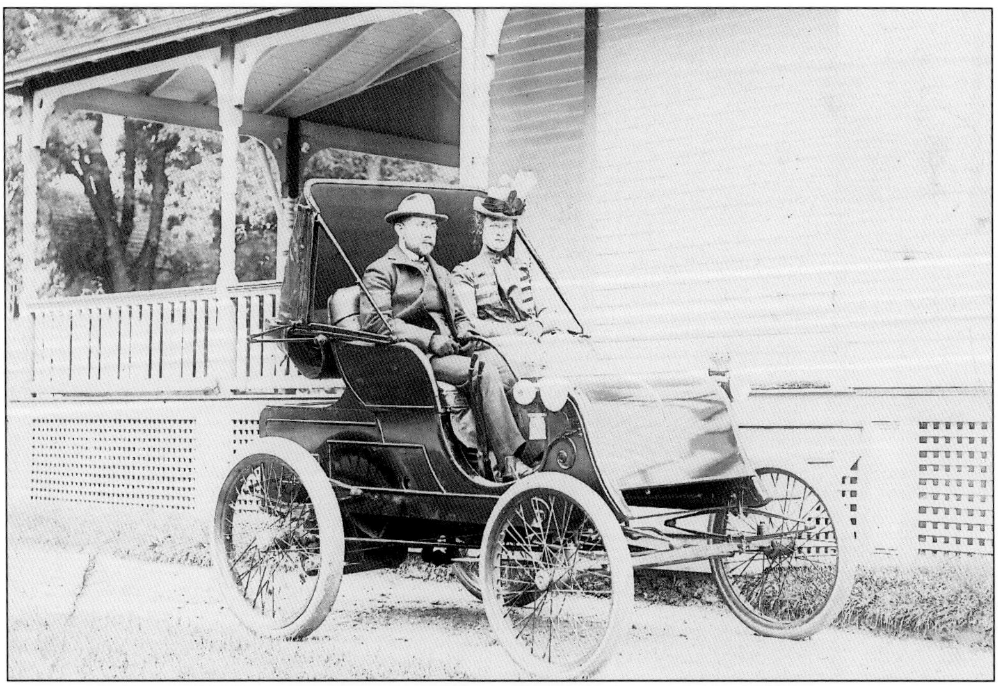

A very early view of an automobile, possibly an electric one, *c*. 1901. The passengers are Ezra Parker and Marietta Cox outside Maryanne's house on Route 9. Note the handle rudder used to steer this automobile.

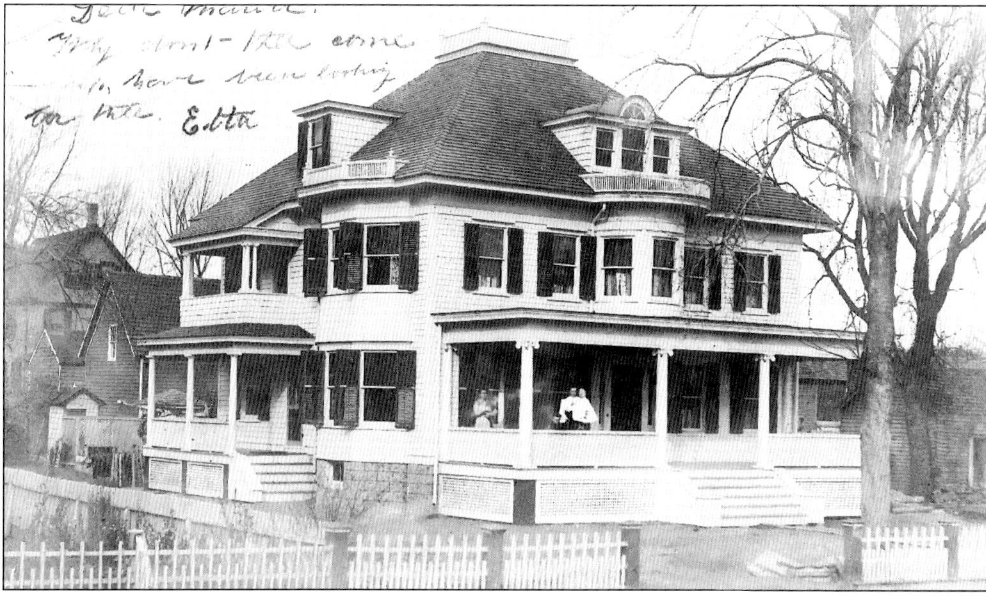

A 1904 postcard view of the Cox House, which was one of the largest and most prestigious homes in the area. The house still stands today at the same location on Route 9.

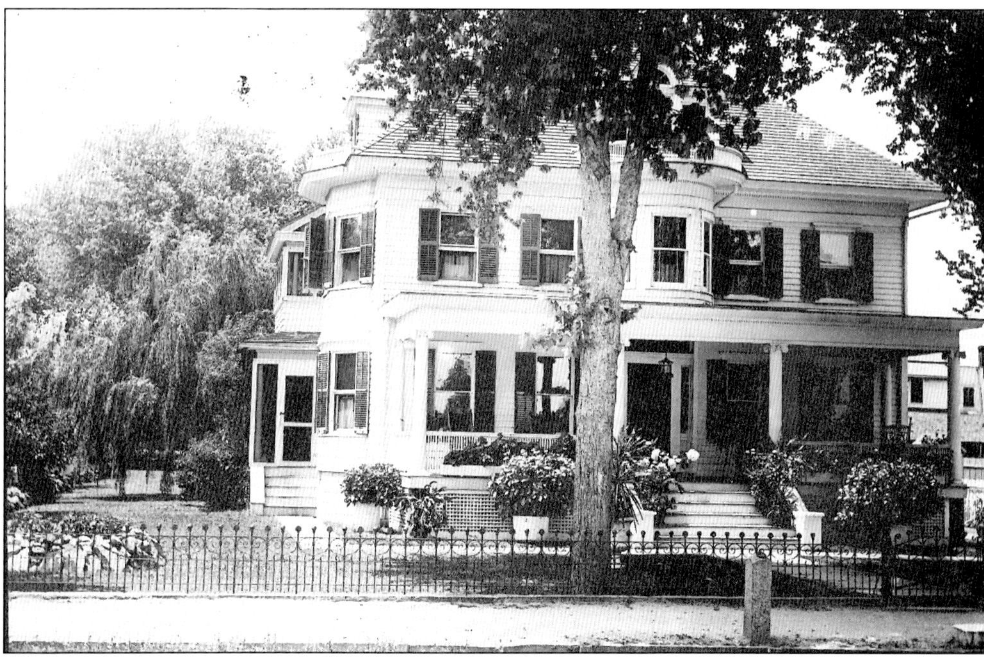

A later view of the Cox House, complete with a wrought-iron fence, around 1910. Today the building is in use as a cultural center.

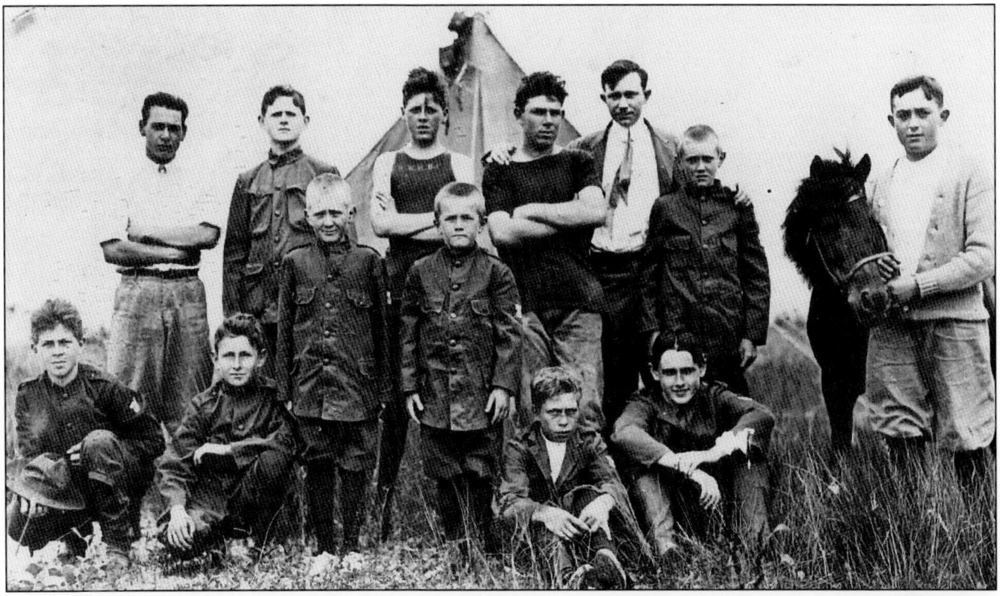

A 1912 image of the first Boy Scout troop in Barnegat taken in the meadows at the bay. Pictured are Van Dyke Connover (in the white shirt), George Gaskell, Horace Sprague, Ralph Cranmer, Al Kelly, Ambrose Cox, David Conrad (with the pony), Cooper Conrad, Buck Ridgeway, Luther Cox, Charles Bennett, Fred L. Bahr, and Howard Rutter.

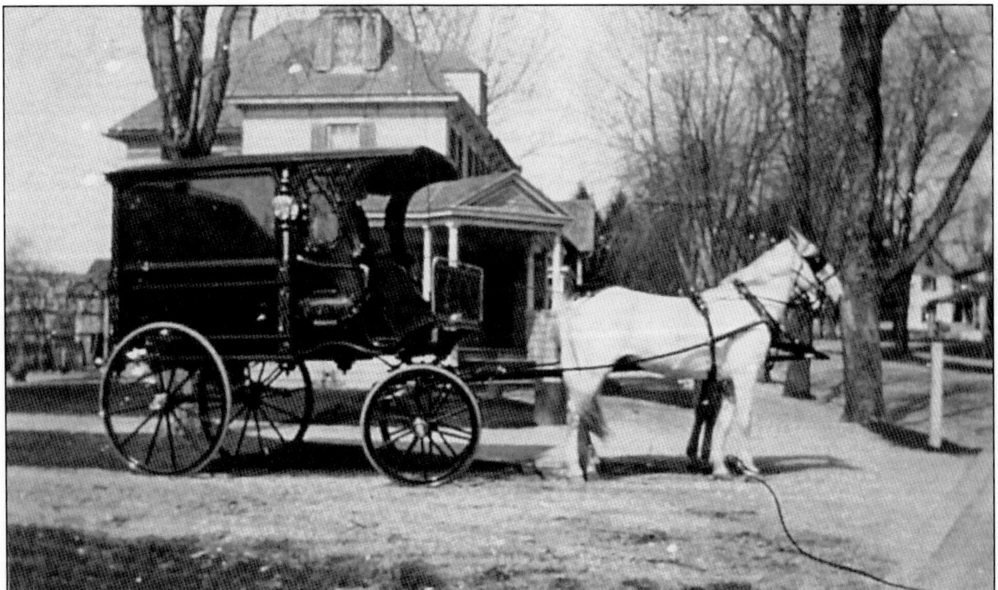

A c. 1916 horse-drawn hearse. The photograph was taken at the corner of Railroad Avenue and West Bay Avenue. Undertaker Job Edwards was a common sight around town. A little-known fact was that a white horse team was used for the funerals of the young, and a black team for those of the old.

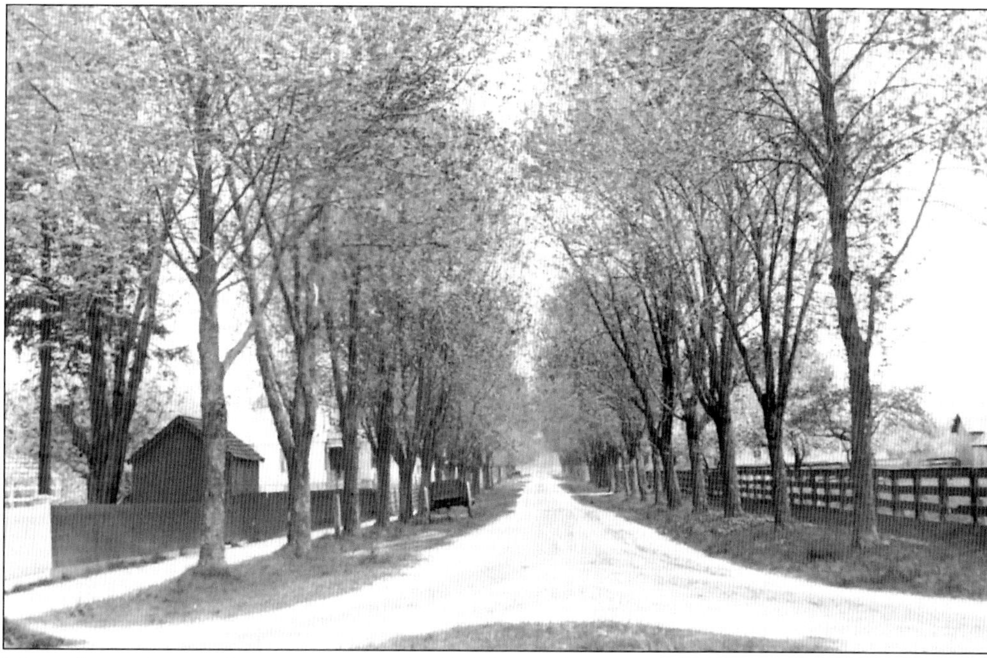

View of an unknown Barnegat street *c.* 1908. Many a dirt-covered road like the one shown here was traveled by residents, farmers, and the occasional visitor on holiday.

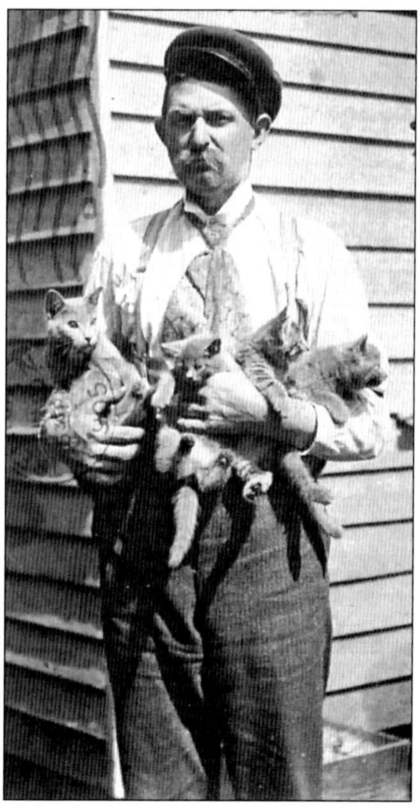

Papa R.G. Collins, photographed around 1905. Ralph was the postmaster of Barnegat around 1910.

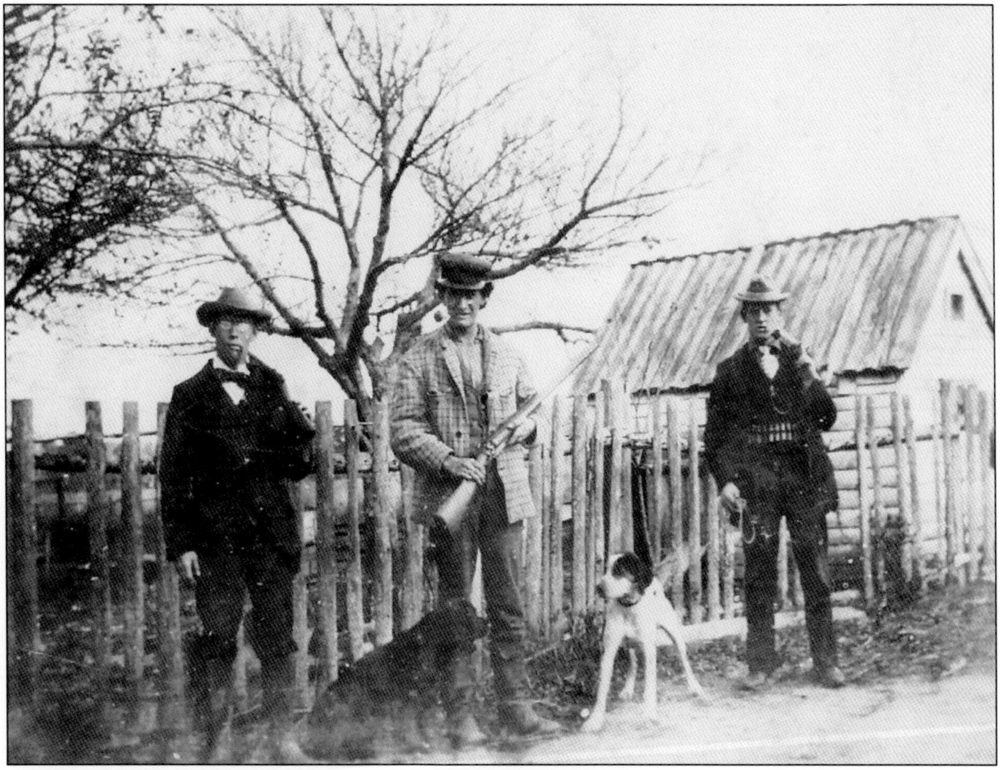

A favorite local pastime. Hunting also became a booming business for area men who served as guides to sport hunters who came by train to hunt the local game. Here a party readies for a day of hunting *c.* 1918.

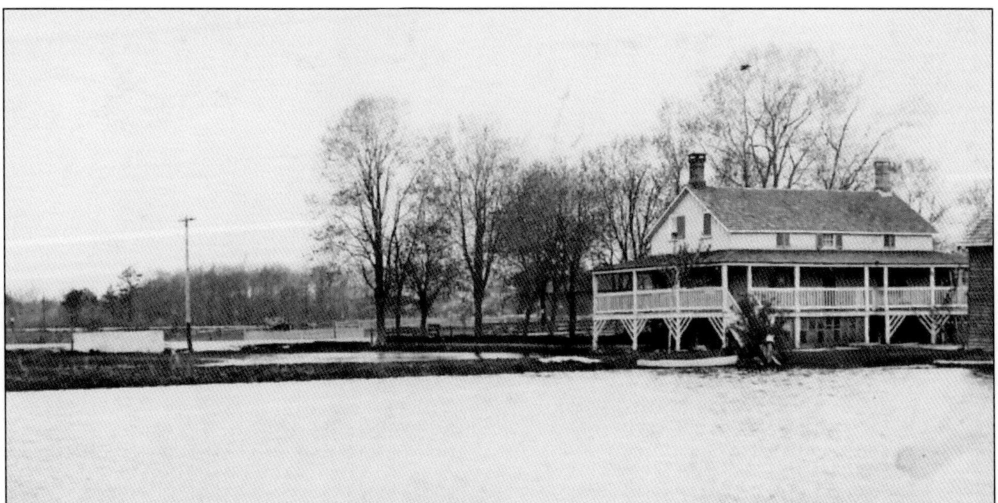

A 1905 view of the Brown Homestead on the corner of Main Street (Route 9) and East Brook Street. The actual living areas of the home are located below ground. The level shown with the railing houses the upstairs bedrooms, and the third floor contains the attic. The Brown children were known to have climbed out of their bedroom windows in the winter to skate on the frozen cranberry bogs nearby.

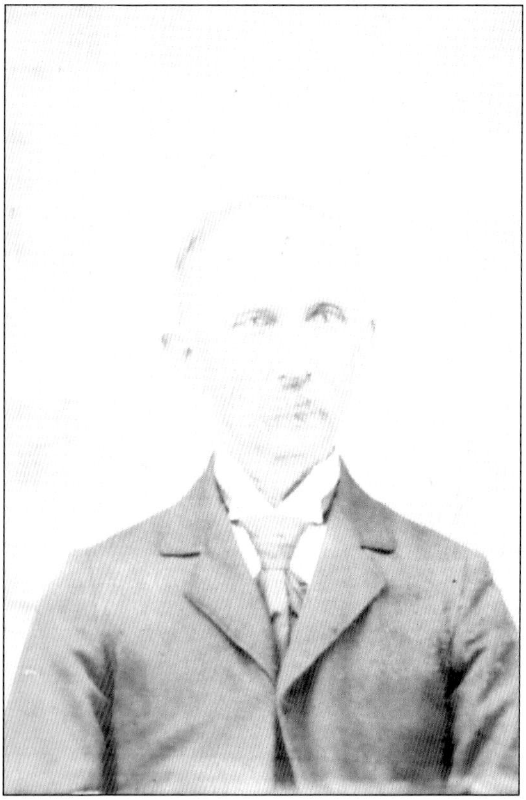

A c. 1899 photograph of A.E. Cranmer. The local name "Cranmer" goes way back in the history of the Barnegat Bay area. Other familiar local names were Cox, Reeves, Birdsall, and Edwards.

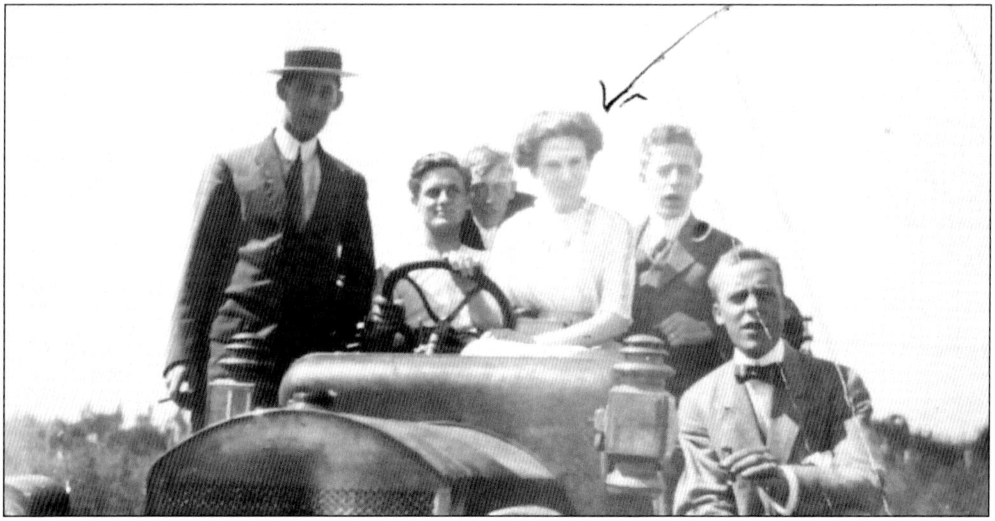

Another view of one of the first automobiles in Barnegat. This view labeled 1910 shows that autos were still an uncommon thing until the 1920s in this area. Those with these cars were considered affluent, and many locals wouldn't trade their horses in for one!

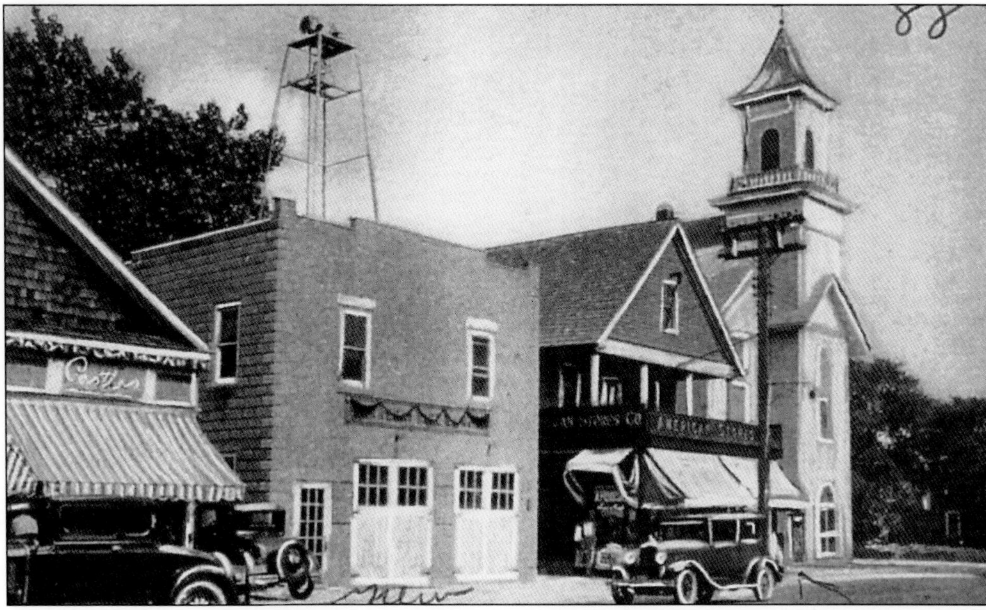

A postcard view of the north side of East Bay Avenue showing Browers drugstore (on the left), the firehouse, and the M.E. church *c.* 1930. This firehouse was the second in Barnegat's history, built in the 1920s and used as a firehouse until 1962.

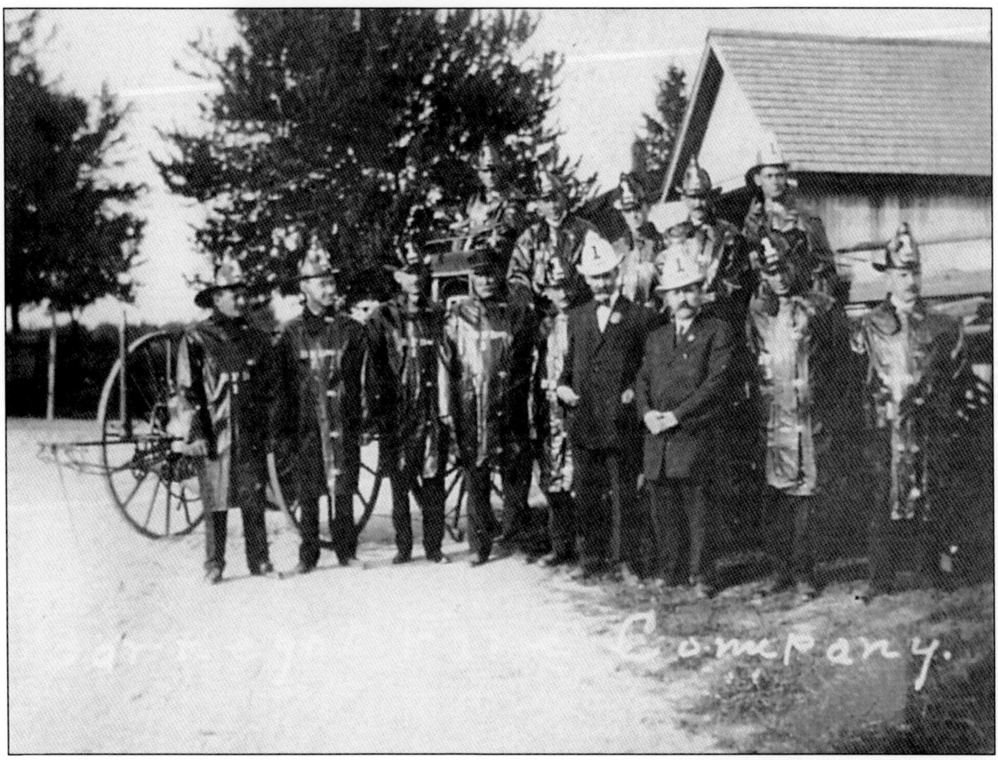

The original Barnegat fire company *c.* 1905. This photograph was taken outside Barnegat's original firehouse on the east side of Birdsall Street, north of Bay Avenue. The building also housed the township offices. Note the hand pumper in the background.

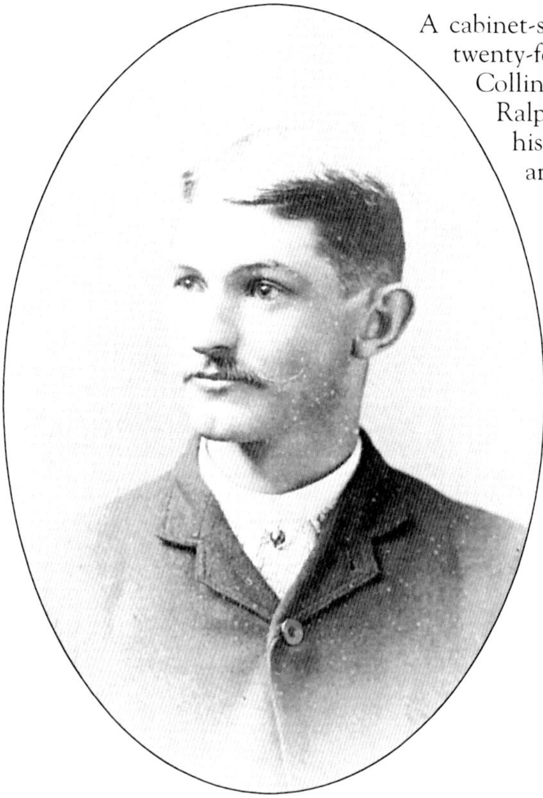

A cabinet-style photograph of Ralph G. Collins, age twenty-four, taken in 1886. Ralph's father, Ralph M. Collins, was postmaster of Barnegat around 1898. Ralph G. Collins, shown here, continued in his father's footsteps and served as postmaster around 1910.

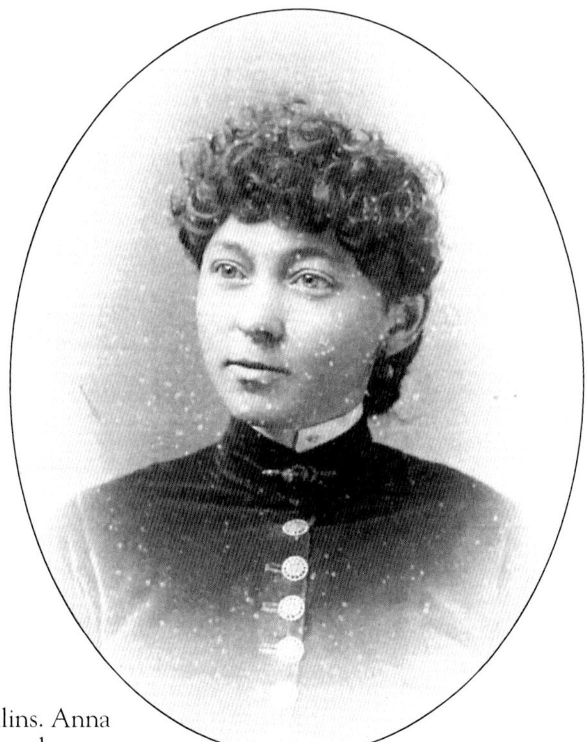

Anna Collins, the wife of Ralph G. Collins. Anna is shown here in an 1887 cabinet photograph.

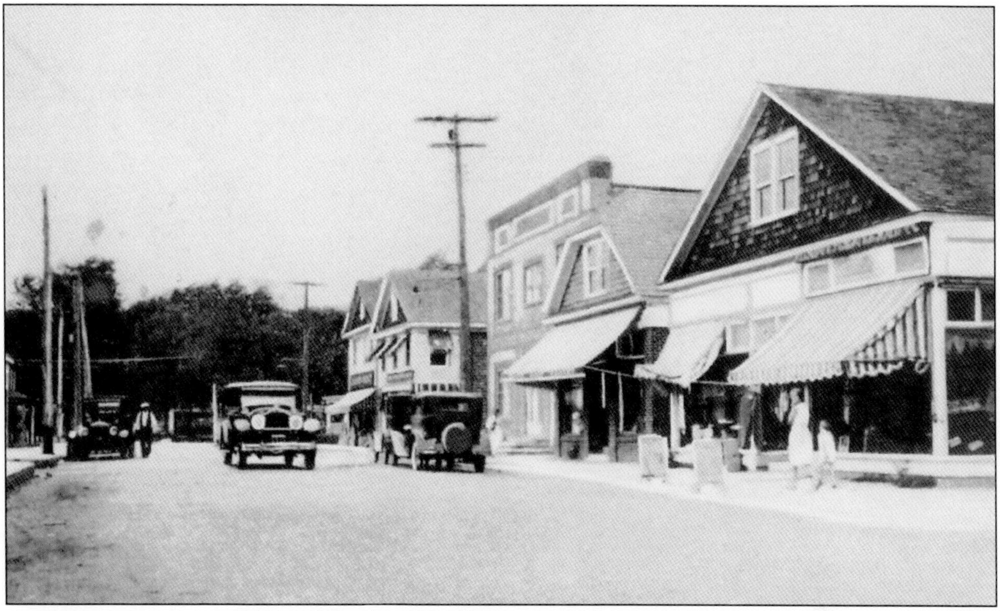

A 1934 postcard view of East Bay Avenue, showing the business (or downtown) district. Many stores were open nights to accommodate the numerous shoppers. Today the architecture remains virtually unchanged.

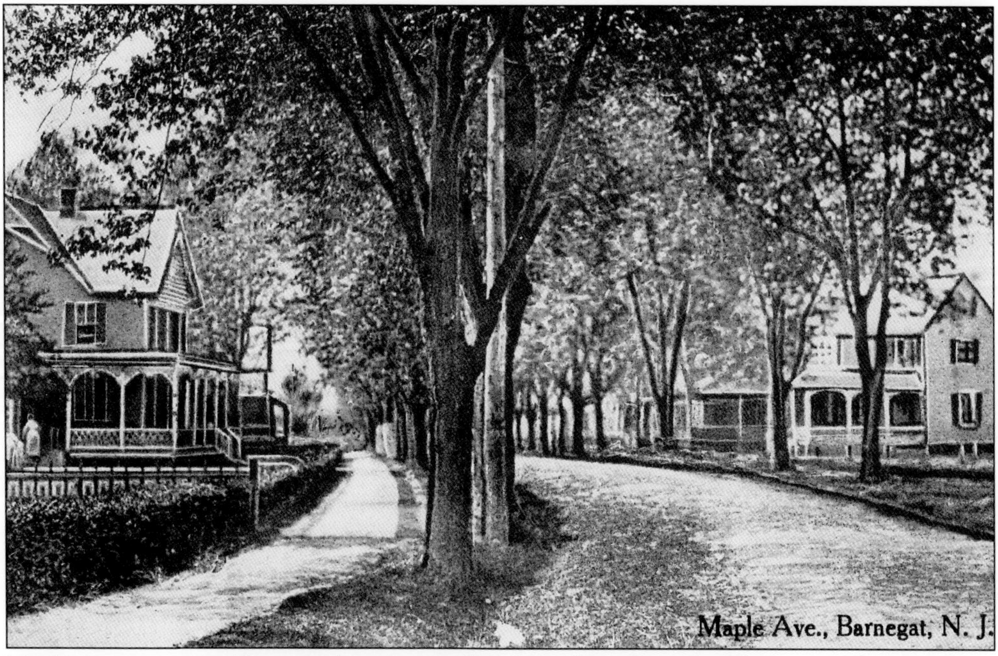

Maple Avenue, one of Barnegat's many tree-lined, residential streets. The avenue features many early examples of Victorian shore area architecture. Many a local seaman lived in these homes. This view was taken c. 1915.

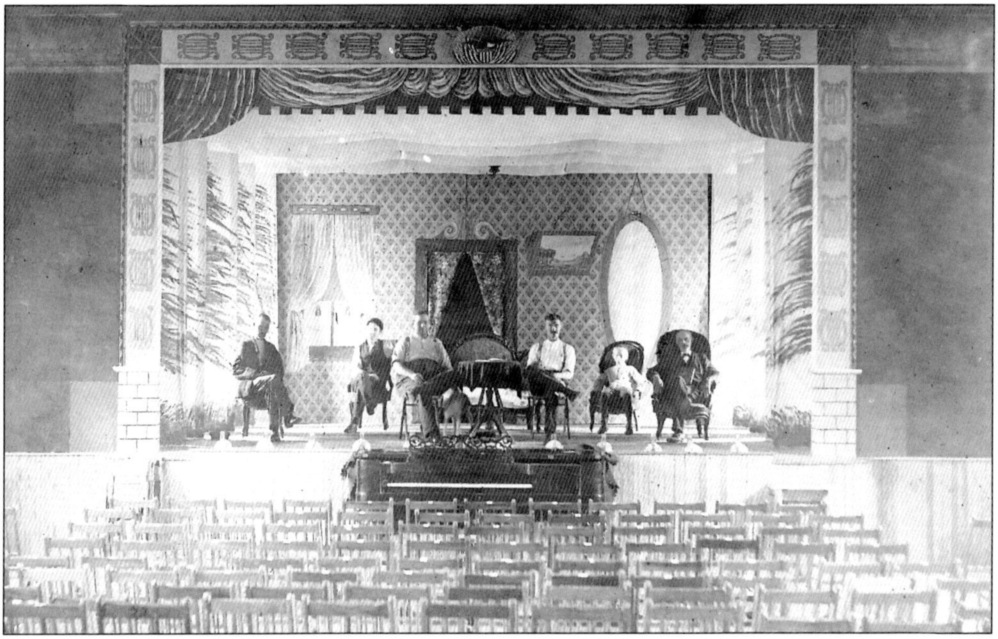

Interior view of the Barnegat Opera House *c.* 1910. This building was built on the east side of North Main Street (Route 9) around 1900 and was used as an opera house until about 1915 when a new entertainment media called "moving pictures" came to town. Identified in this view are Charles Reeves (third from the left) and Jerry Storms (on the extreme right). The building was later modernized in the 1930s and renamed The Park Theatre.

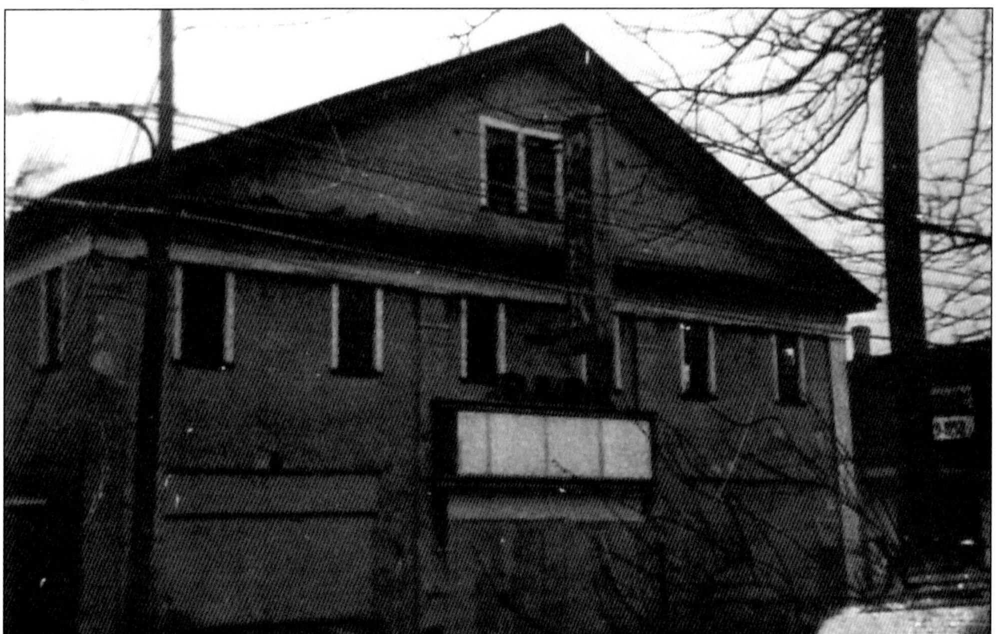

The Park Theatre. Shown here in the 1930s, the theatre building contained a store on either side of the main entrance, apartments on the second level in the front, and the movie theatre in the rear.

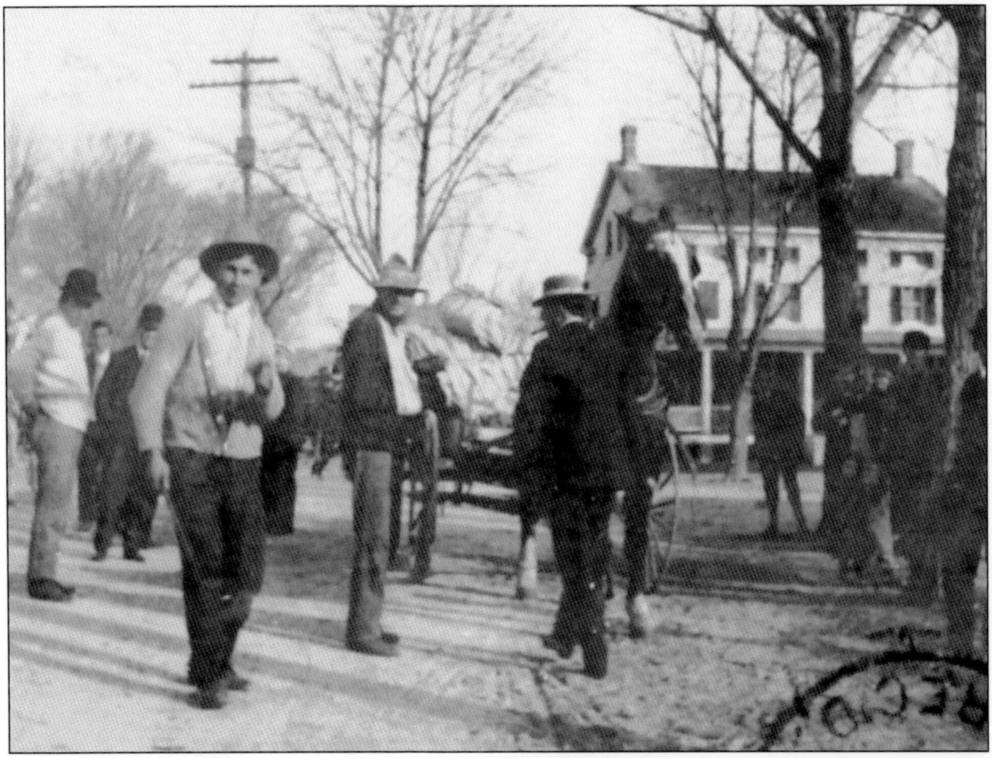

A *c.* 1909 view of "the gypsies" heading south through town on their annual trek. The Almont Inn is shown in the background. Real-photo postcards such as this one capture a particular moment in time.

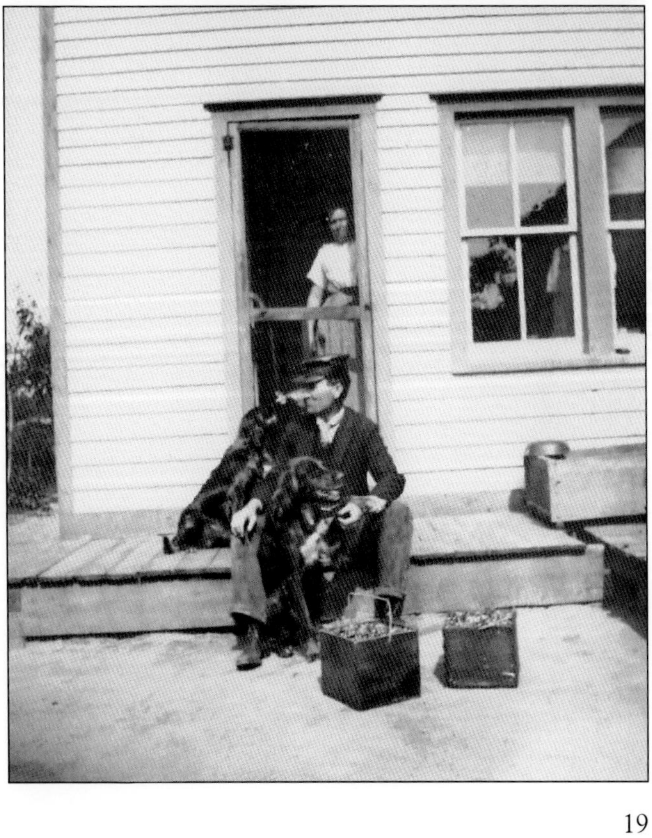

Agricultural income. The harvest and sale of cranberries became a very popular industry in the area. Shown here on the porch of their home are May and William Reeves, c. 1910, with two baskets of local cranberries.

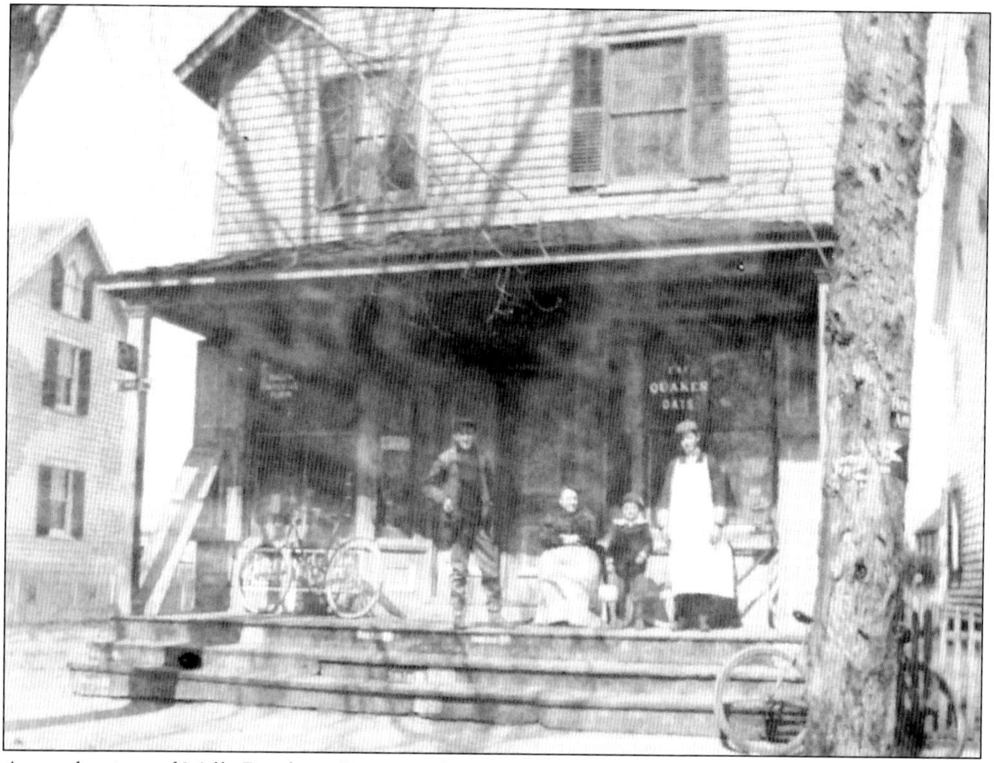

An early view of Mills Brothers Store on the corner of Ridgeway and East Bay Avenue. These general stores carried a little of everything from hardware to clothing to groceries.

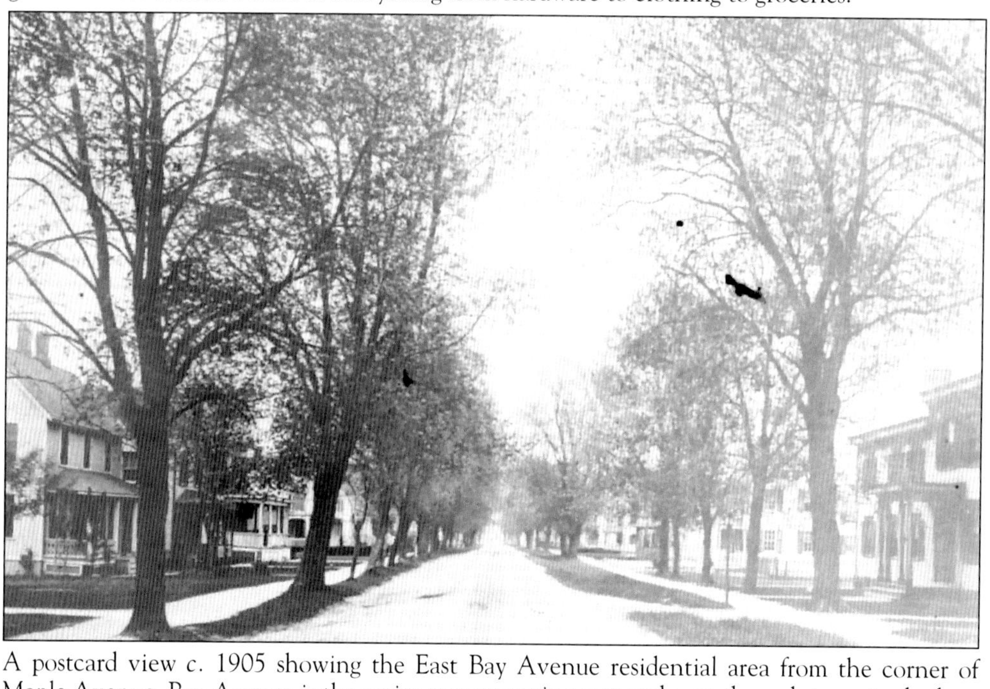

A postcard view c. 1905 showing the East Bay Avenue residential area from the corner of Maple Avenue. Bay Avenue is the major street running east and west through town to the bay. Note the various styles of architecture still preserved today by caring residents.

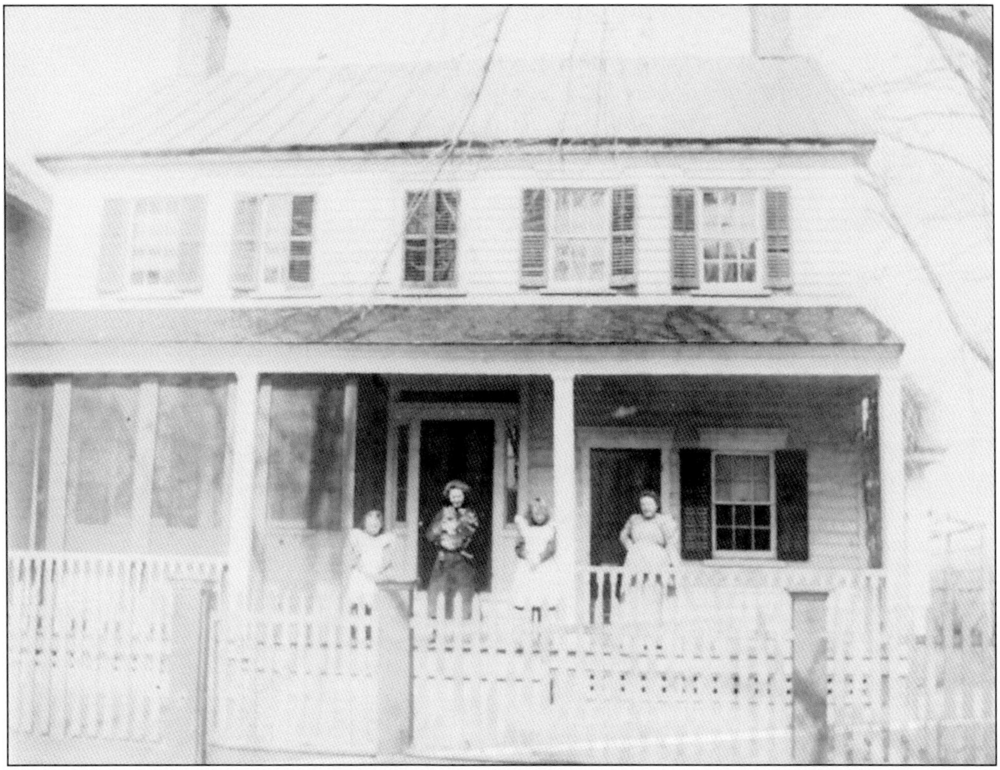

The home of George and Carrie Hollingsworth. This is a typical Barnegat home with a wide porch and two fireplaces, one placed at each end of the house for heat and cooking purposes.

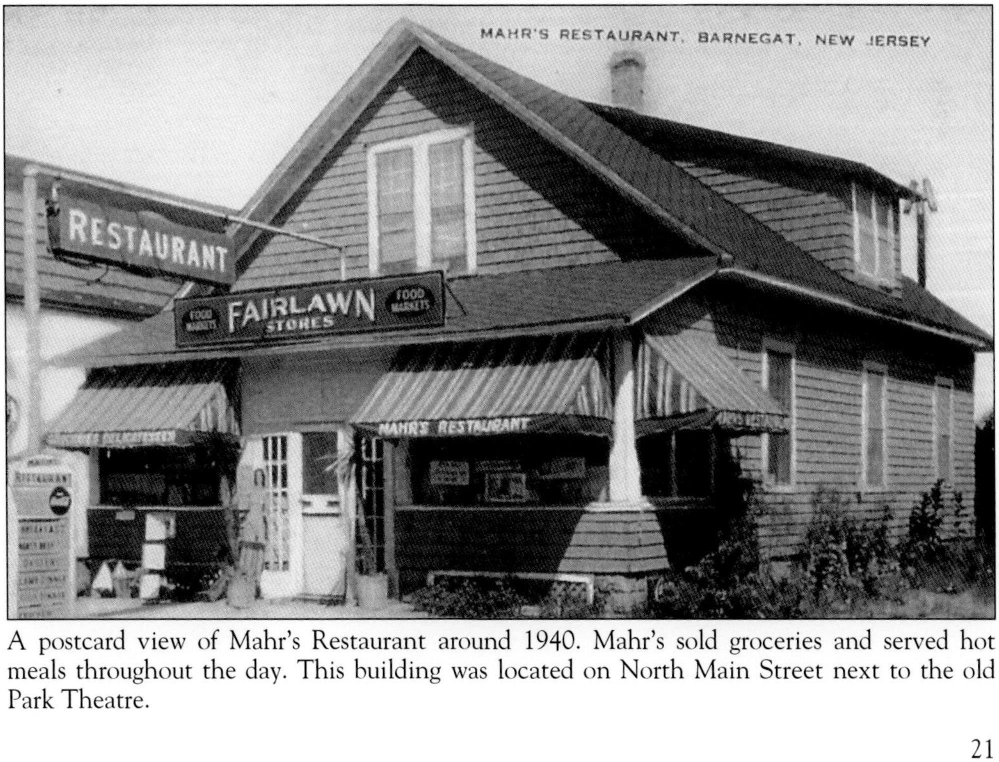

A postcard view of Mahr's Restaurant around 1940. Mahr's sold groceries and served hot meals throughout the day. This building was located on North Main Street next to the old Park Theatre.

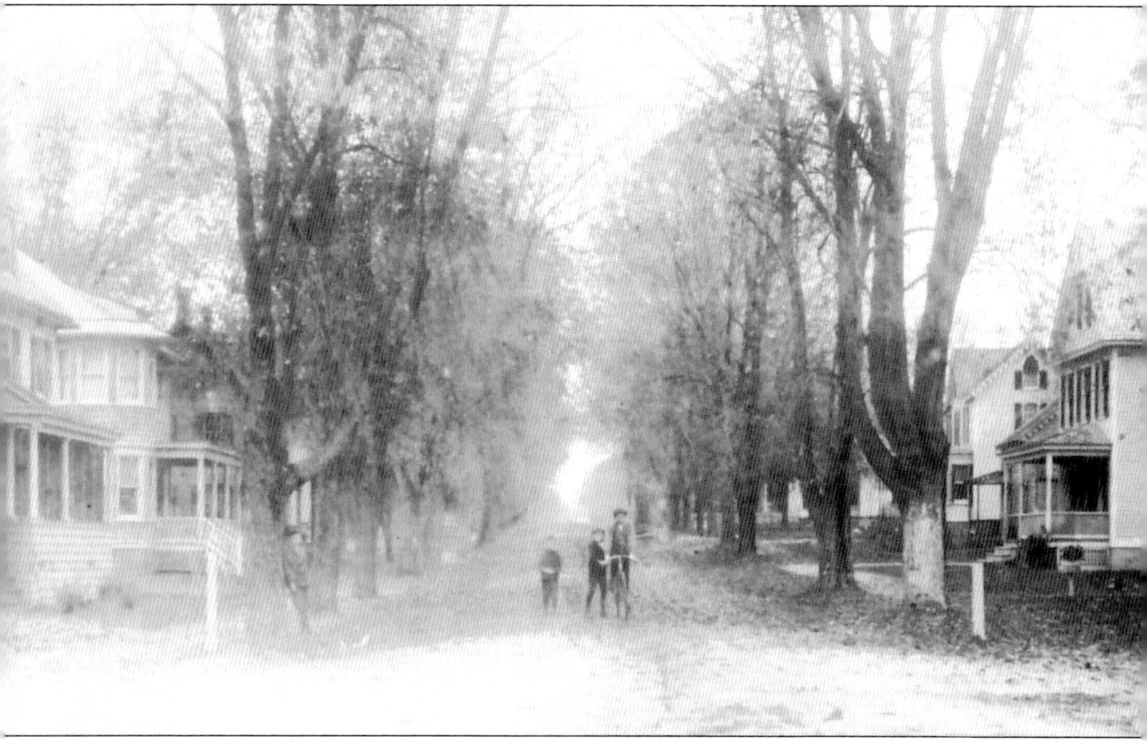

Bay Street, also known as Bay Avenue, *c.* 1909. The photographer was looking west from Route 9. The train station is at the immediate right, out of view.

Two

Goin' Downtown

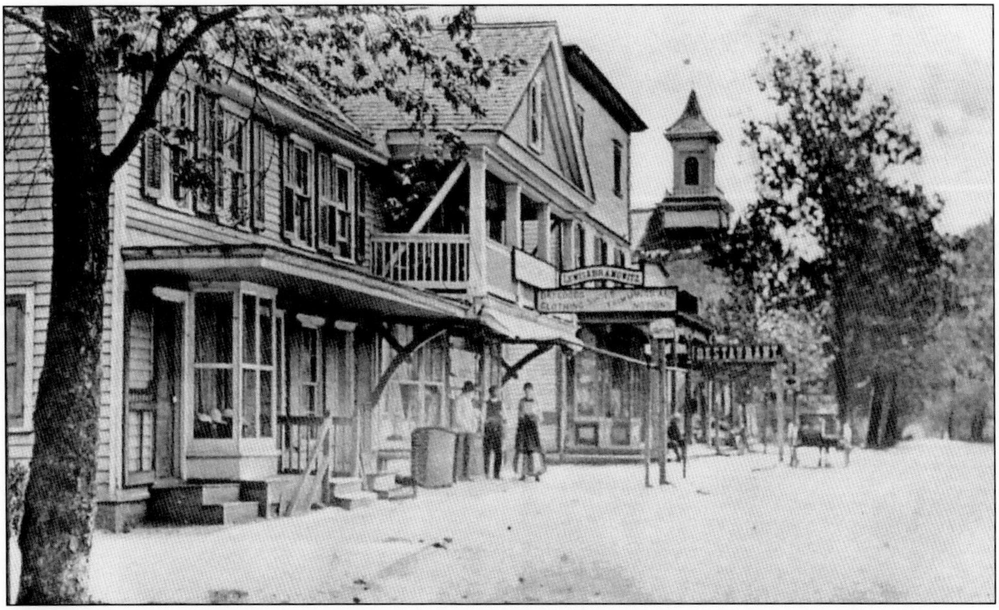

The Barnegat business district around 1916, looking east from Main Street (Route 9). This area was the center of commerce for the town, complete with dry goods stores, a grocer, a butcher, and other necessary merchants.

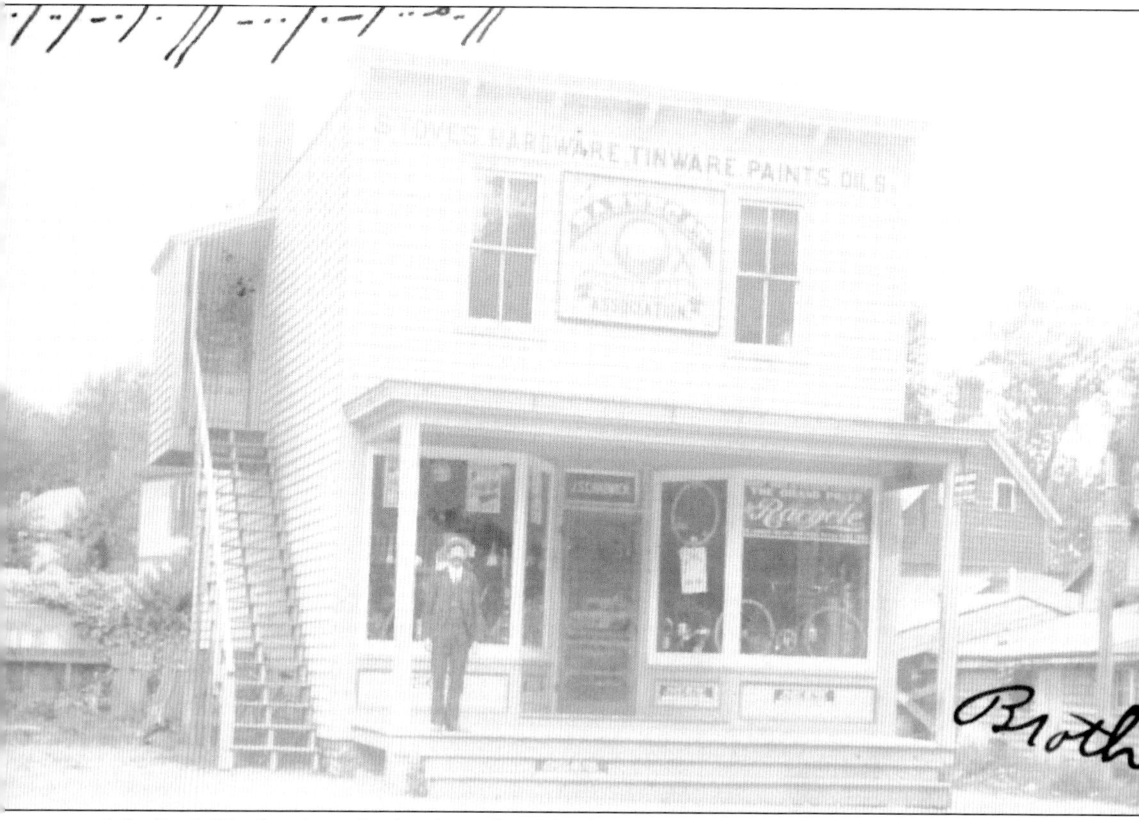

J.S. (Joe) Chadwick at the hardware/bicycle shop *c.* 1905. All forms of household necessities could be found here. Items included stoves, hardware, pots, pans, and paints. This store still stands today on the west side of Bay Avenue. Note the location of the Barnegat Athletic Association upstairs.

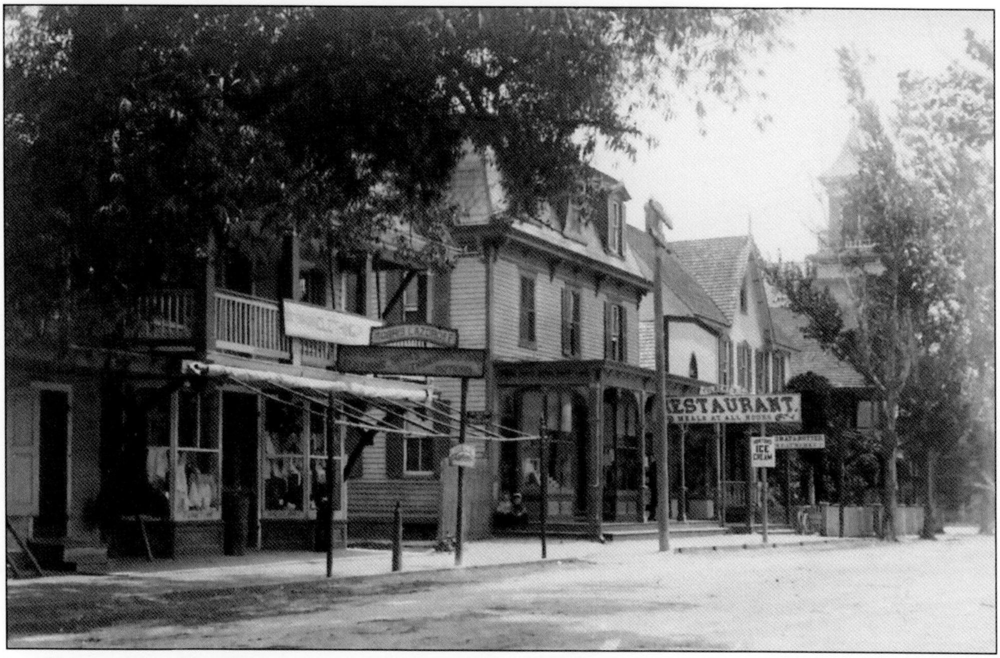

Looking east on East Bay Avenue. Around 1908, we can clearly see Lazaroffs clothing store, the Masonic Temple, Tolbert's restaurant, and Gray and Rutters meat market. Tolbert's restaurant featured "Meals at all Hours."

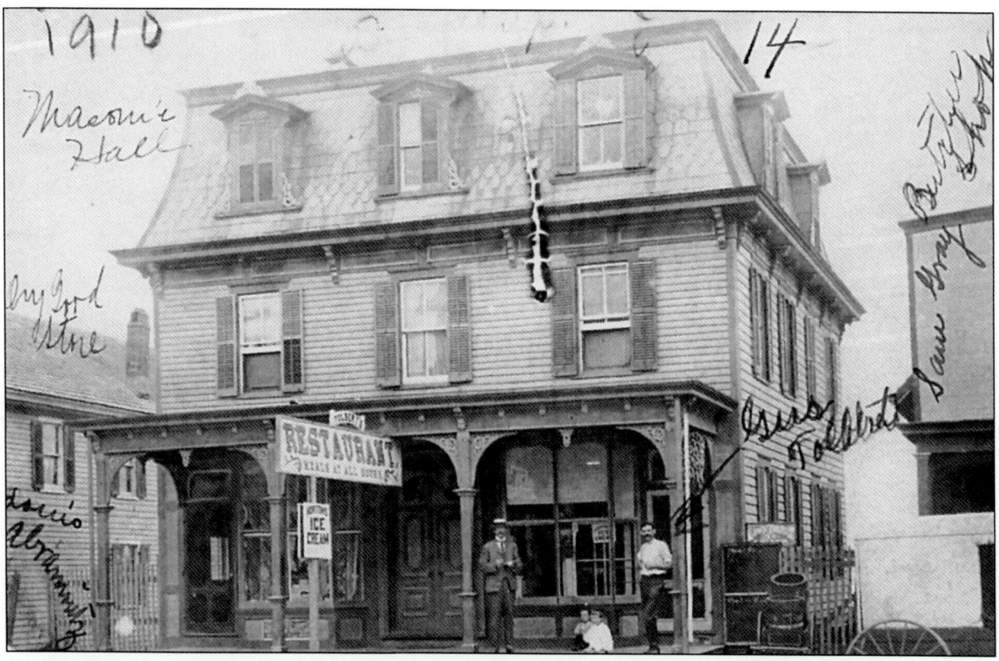

Gus Tolbert (right) on the steps of his restaurant c. 1910. The Masonic Temple held meetings upstairs. At left is Abromowitz's Dry Goods store and at right is Sam Gray's Butcher Shop and wagon.

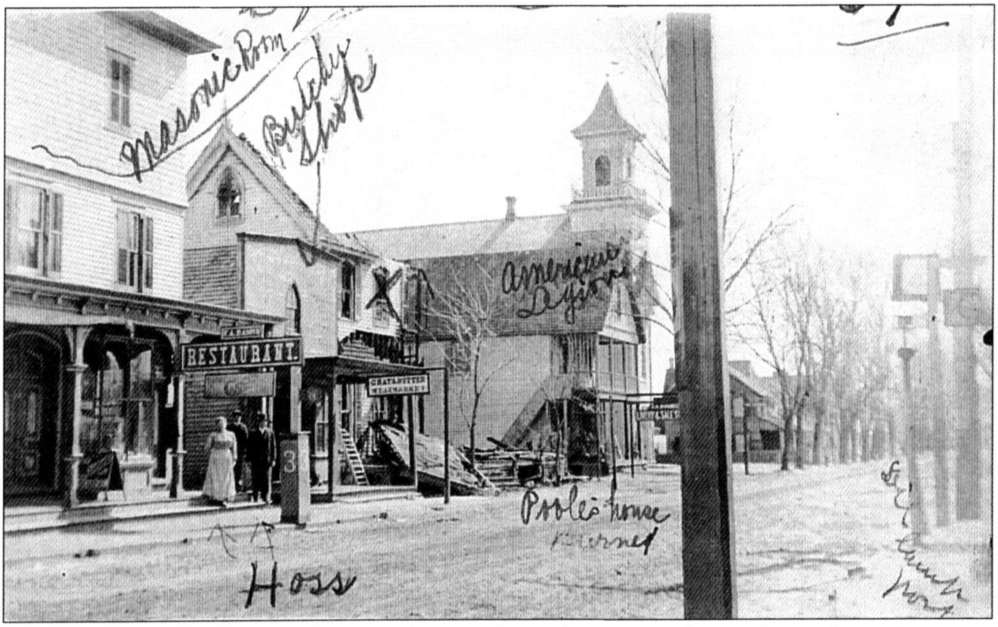

Another view of the East Bay business district after a devastating fire at the Predmore house on March 4, 1912. Note the oil lamppost on the right. Such devices provided much-needed light at night, as most businesses were open late.

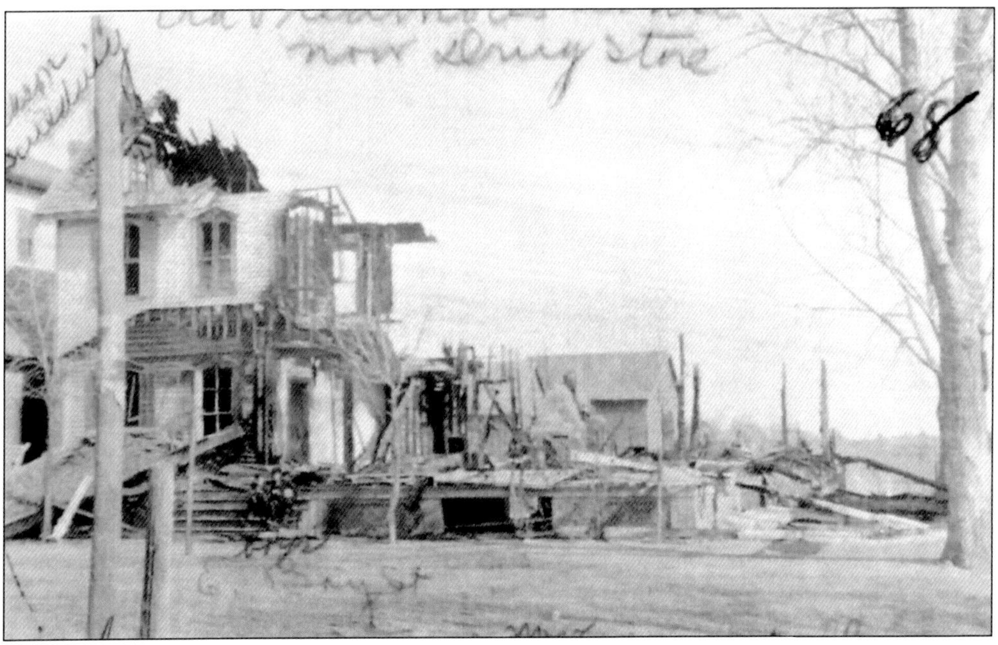

A closer view of the fire damage with the butcher shop shown on the left. The site was cleared and a drugstore built. Later an ice cream parlor and a firehouse were added to this site.

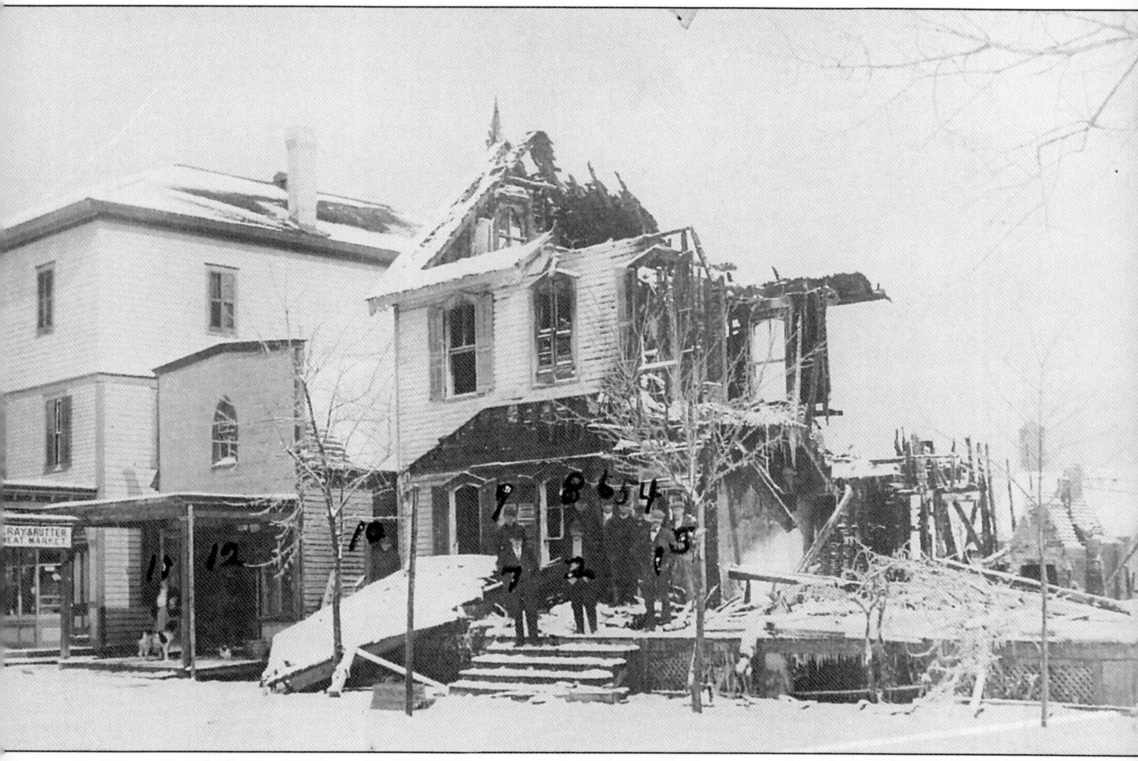

A valiant fire-fighting effort. Henry Pole occupied the old Predmore house at the time of the fire. It happened at 2 am on the morning of March 4, 1912. The small crew of the Barnegat Fire Company was no match for the blaze with their hand pumper and bucket brigade. Wooden structures like these were prone to fire, with candles and gas lamps being used to illuminate the homes at night.

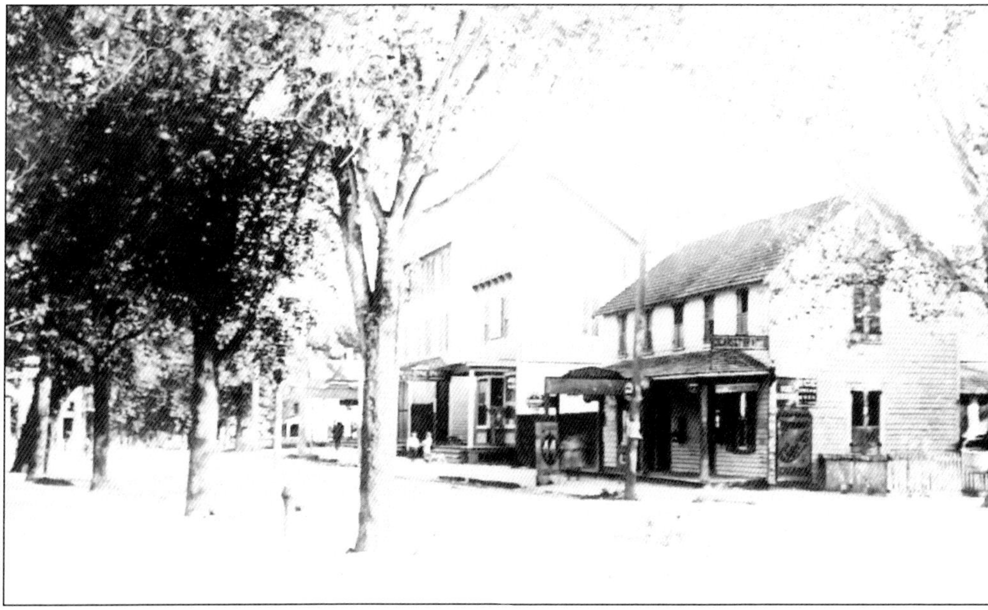

A *c.* 1910 postcard view, this one taken by a Howell photographer named Merriman. Merriman traveled via early automobile throughout Monmouth and Ocean Counties taking local shots and selling them on postcards to anyone who would buy them. This view shows the corner of Main and Bay Streets featuring Elberson's restaurant.

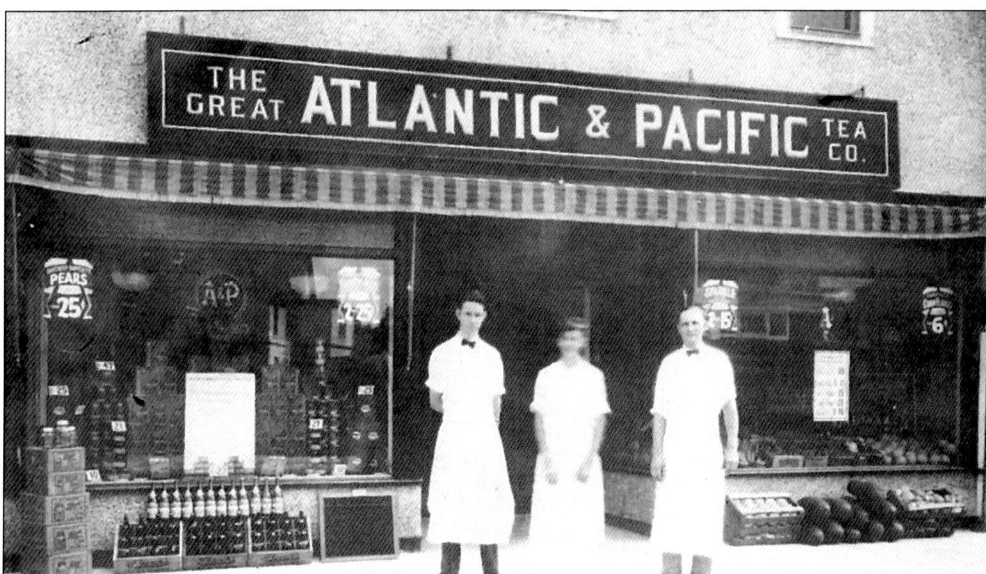

The Great Atlantic and Pacific Tea Company, or A&P, on the north side of East Bay Avenue near Main Street (Route 9). Stores such as this prided themselves on having the best window and sidewalk displays, as seen here.

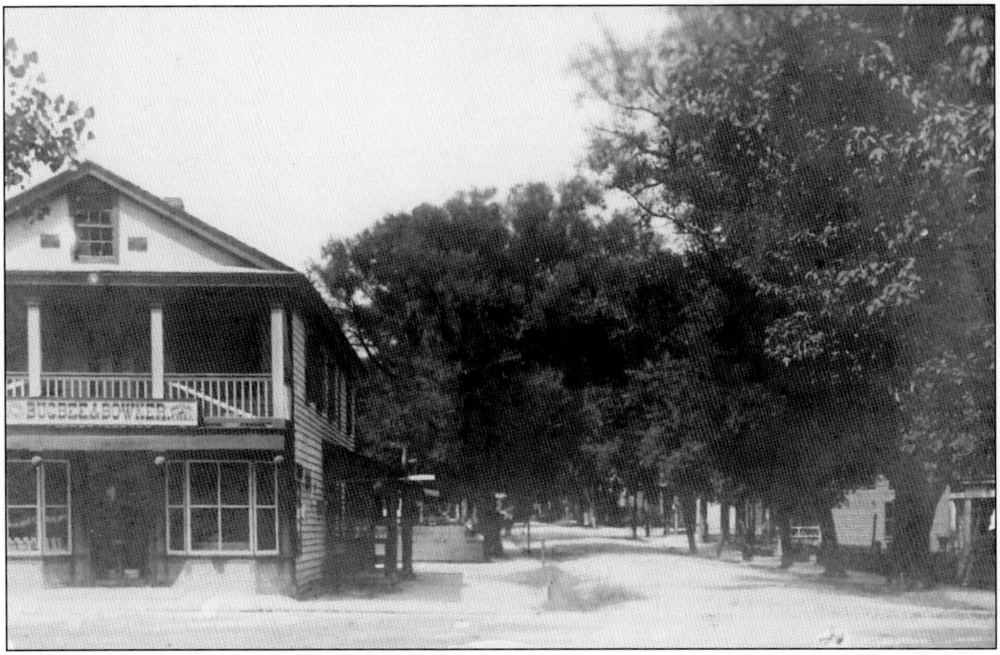

The Bugbee and Bowkers Store, *c.* 1912, on the corner of West Bay Street and Main Street (Route 9). This store featured all types of groceries and provisions. Today the building remains, altered slightly, and serves as an antique center.

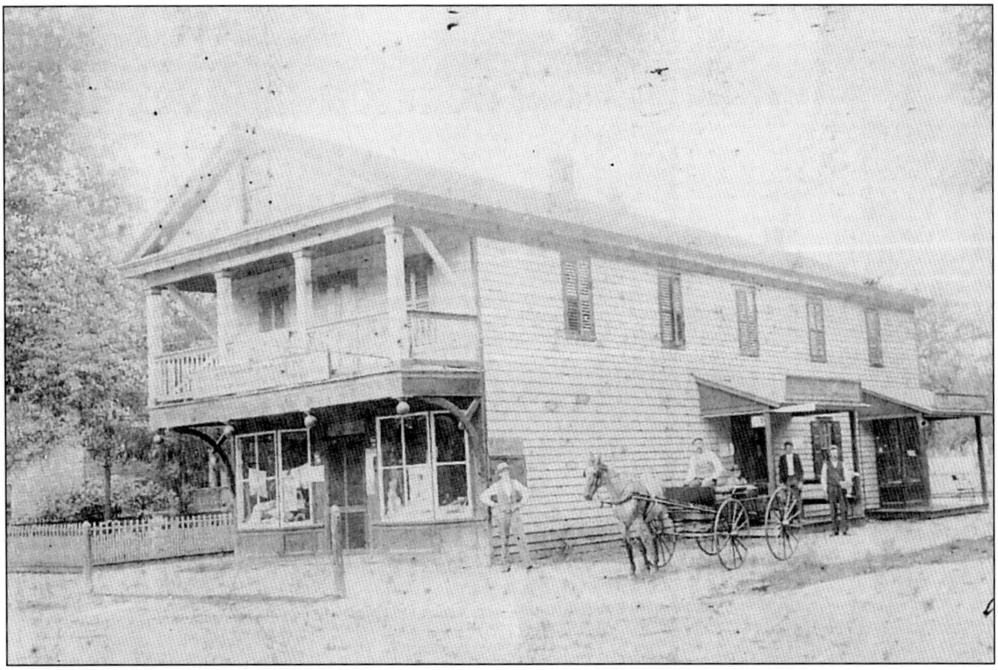

Another earlier view, this one taken around 1900, of the Bugbee and Bowkers store. This building was built around 1880 and originally housed the Collins & Gulicks store. Deliveries were made via buckboard wagon.

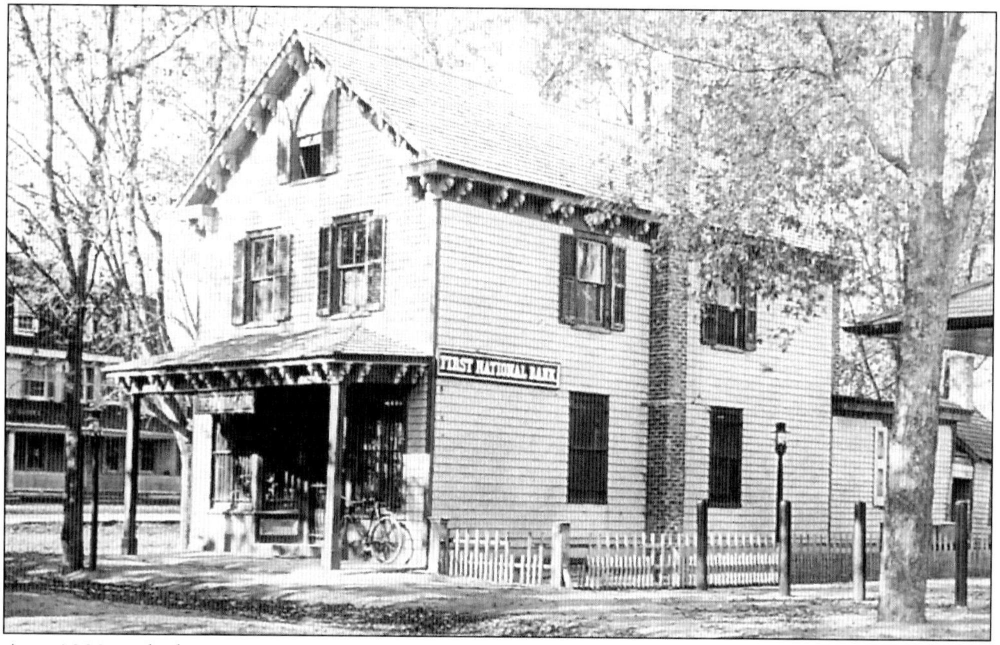

A c. 1908 real-photo postcard of the First National Bank. The bank started in January 1907 inside the Collins & Gulicks store. They then moved into this new building on the corner of West Bay and Railroad Avenues around 1908. The bank remained in this building until a new one was built on the same site in 1914. This building was moved to Cedar Street and is still used as a private residence.

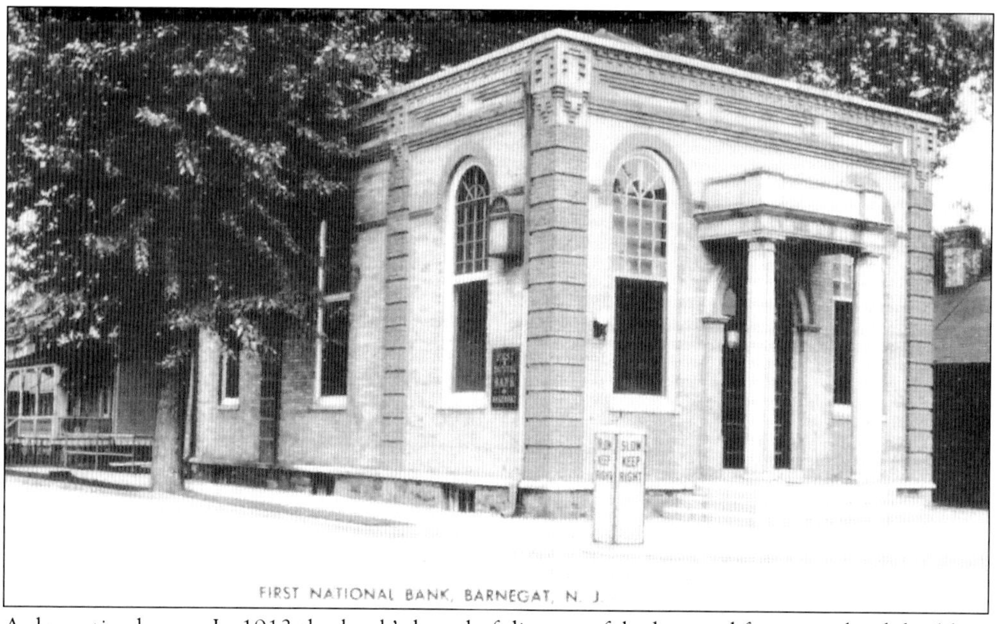

A dramatic change. In 1913 the bank's board of directors felt the need for a new bank building and in February of 1914 approved a bid for a more modern structure to be built on the same site. This location was ideal, as it was situated right in between two railroad depots and one block from the center of town. Work began in the spring of 1914 and the new bank building remained in use until 1975.

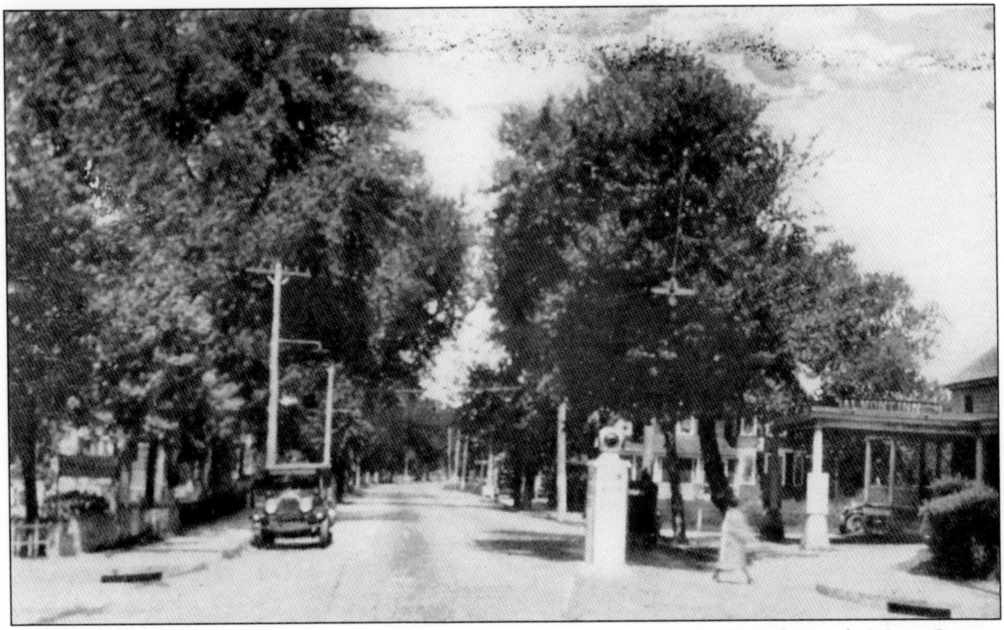

A 1929 view of the Almont Inn at the intersection of Bay Avenue and North Main Street. Note the very early traffic light on the concrete pedestal in the center of the road.

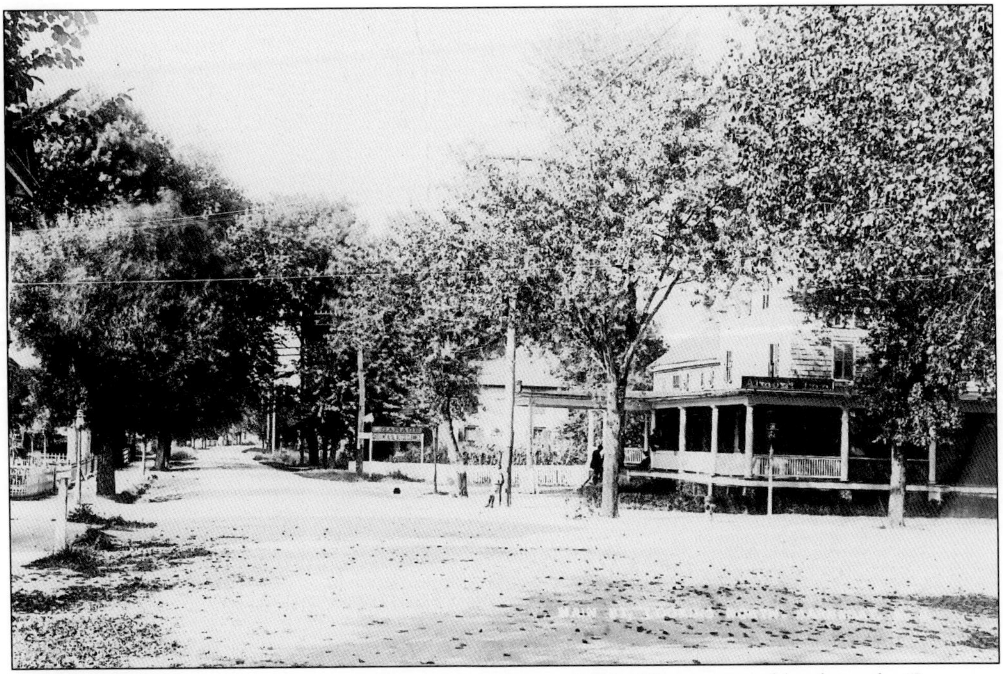

Another early view of the same intersection, taken c. 1910. The postcard back reads, "I ran my motorcar 80 miles here today, going home tomorrow, never had a more glorious time!"

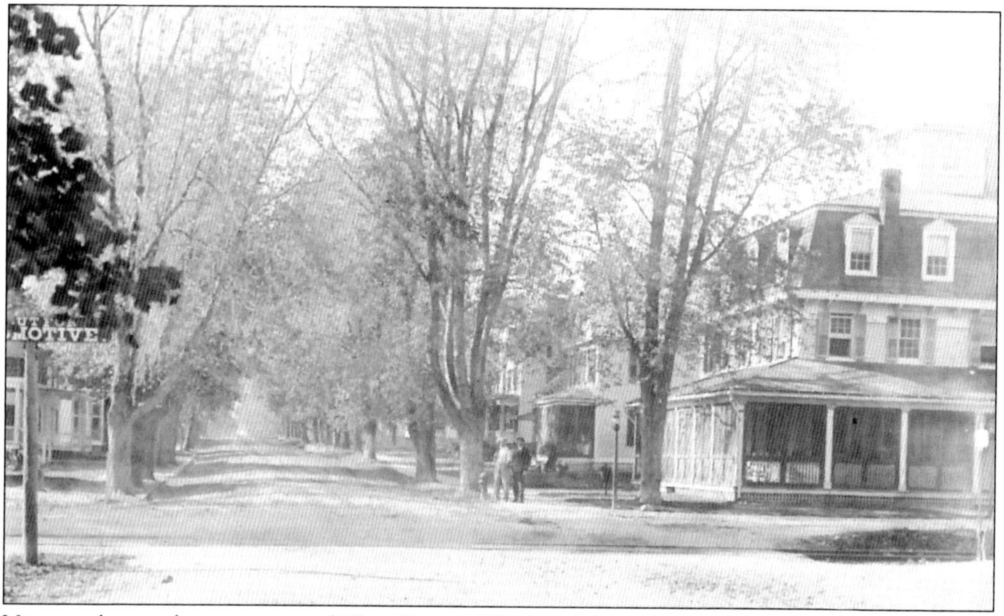

View at the northwest corner of West Bay and Railroad Avenues c. 1909. The Clarence House Hotel at right represented the period of the Gay Nineties in Barnegat. One of many hotels in town, it catered to sport hunters and overnight train patrons. It was later renamed the Hotel Barnegat.

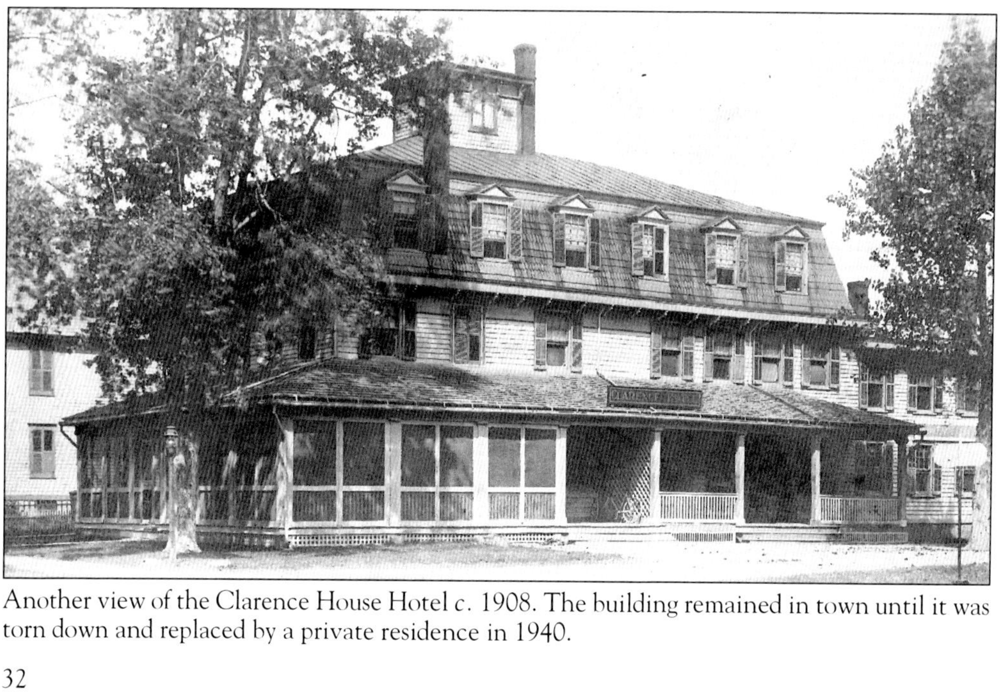

Another view of the Clarence House Hotel c. 1908. The building remained in town until it was torn down and replaced by a private residence in 1940.

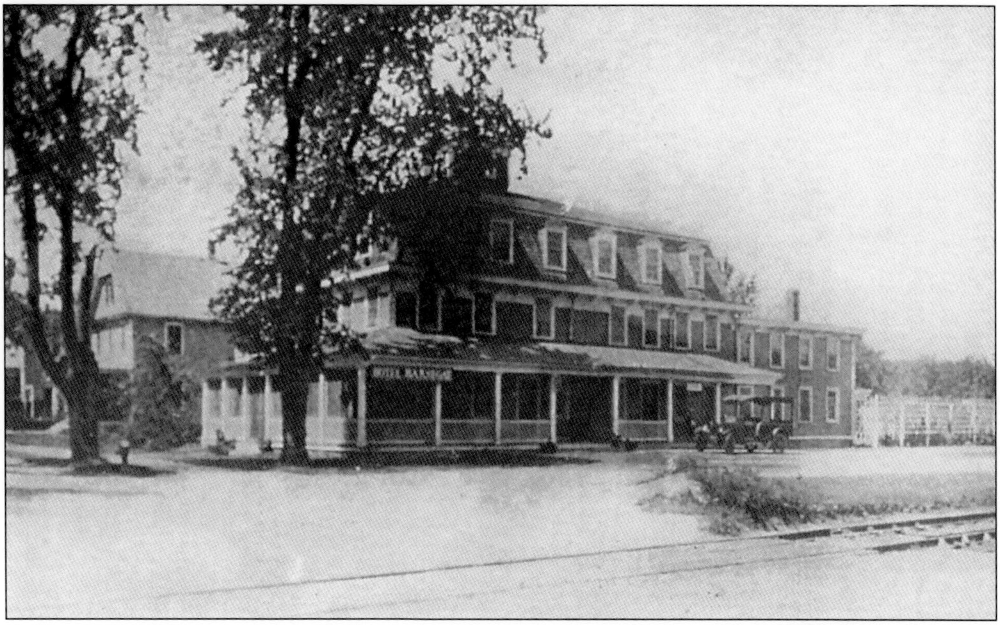

A later postcard view of the Clarence House Hotel, here called the Hotel Barnegat. The train tracks in the foreground belonged to the Tuckerton Railroad.

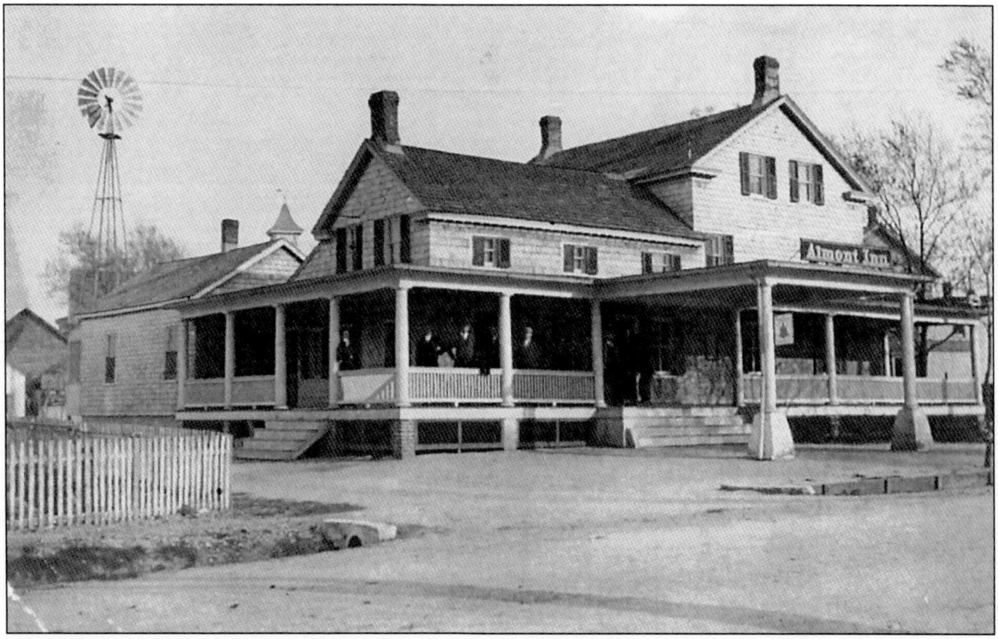

The Almont Inn, one of several hotels in town, *c.* 1910. The inn stood on the northeast corner of East Bay Avenue and North Main Street (Route 9). It was built in 1820, and was known as the Mullen house. Note the early windmill in the background.

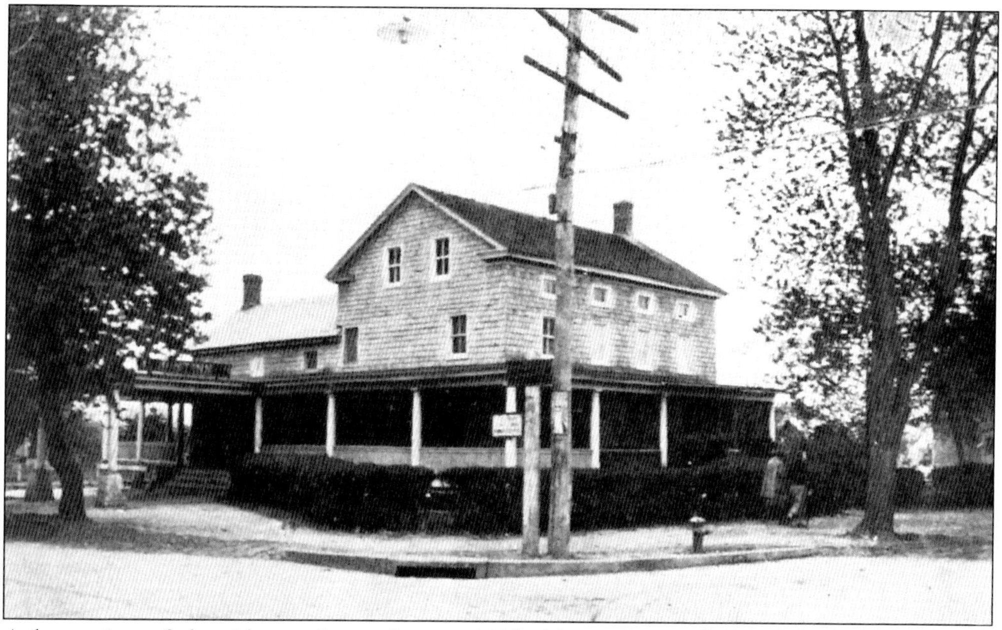

A later view of the Almont Inn, taken *c.* 1920. Many visiting hunters stayed here during duck-hunting seasons, which typically lasted from October through December and from March through April. Rooms could be had for a few dollars a day.

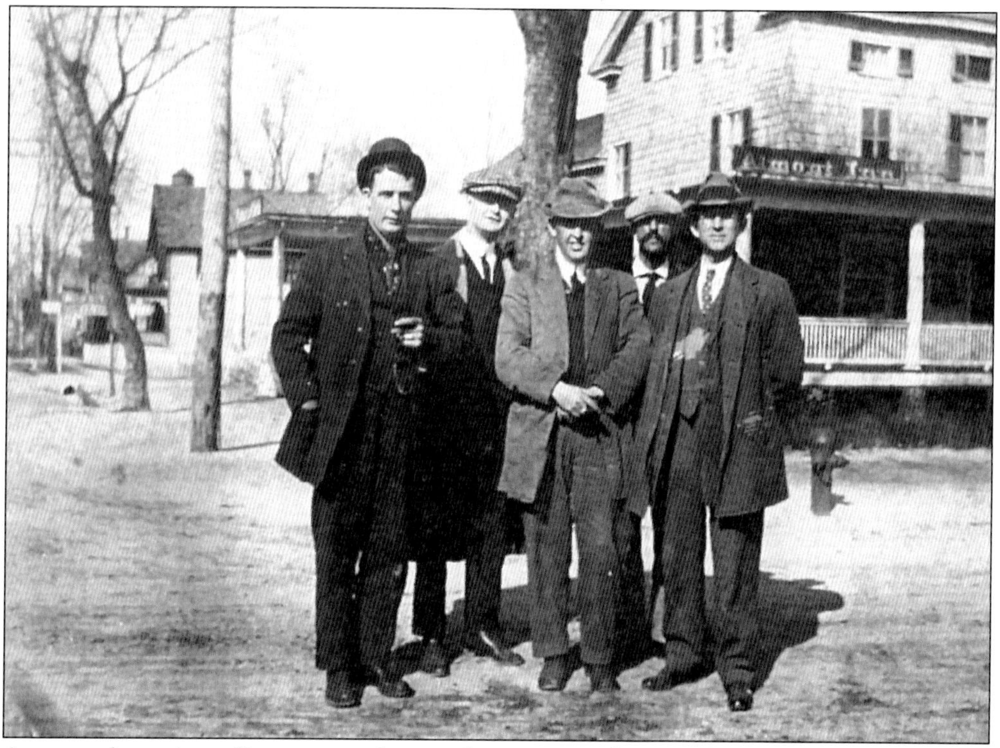

A group of prominent Barnegat residents gathering to catch up on the news of the day. Shown from left to right are Charlie Thompson (Central Railroad engineer), John Carter (coffee dealer), John Russell (salesman), Seal Reeves (jitney driver), and George Hopper (barber).

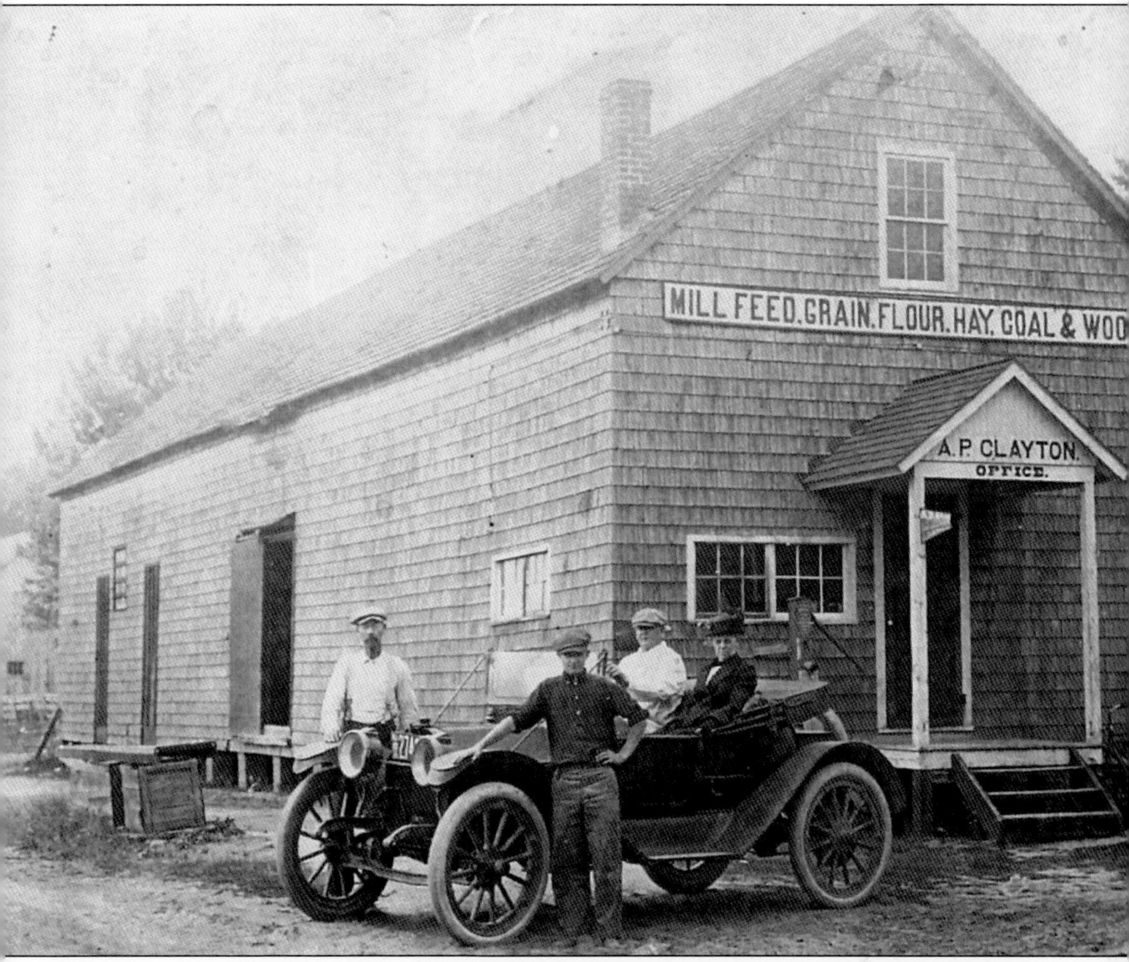

Early view around 1914 of A.P. Clayton's store located on the corner of West Brook Street and Railroad Avenue. Note the right-hand-drive early automobile and the outfit worn by the driver.

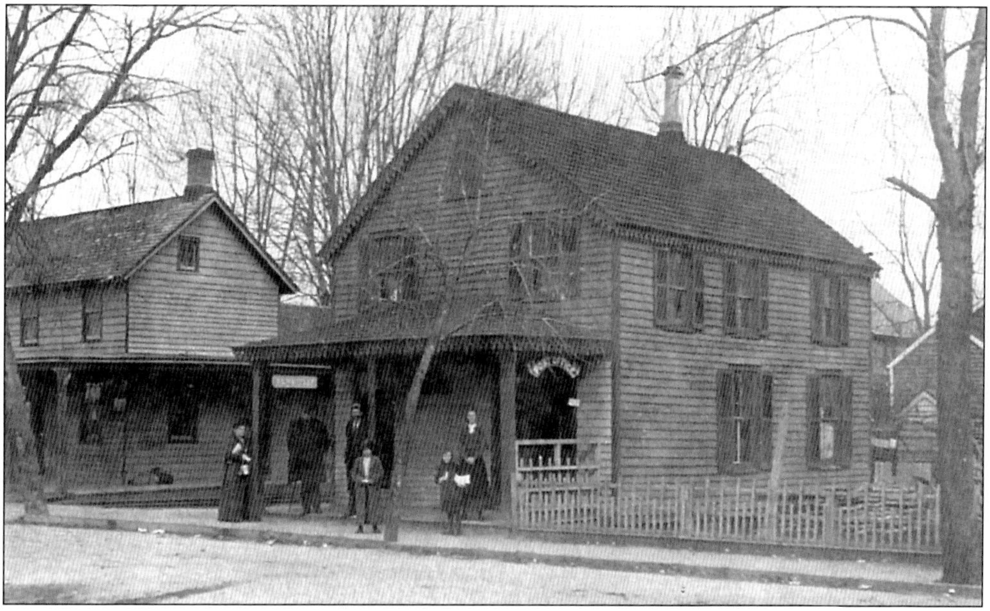

A postcard view of Barnegat's original post office, which was built before the turn of the century. After outgrowing this building, the post office moved to a new structure; this one became a printing office. This *c.* 1905 view also shows the old Central Railroad (CRR) station at left.

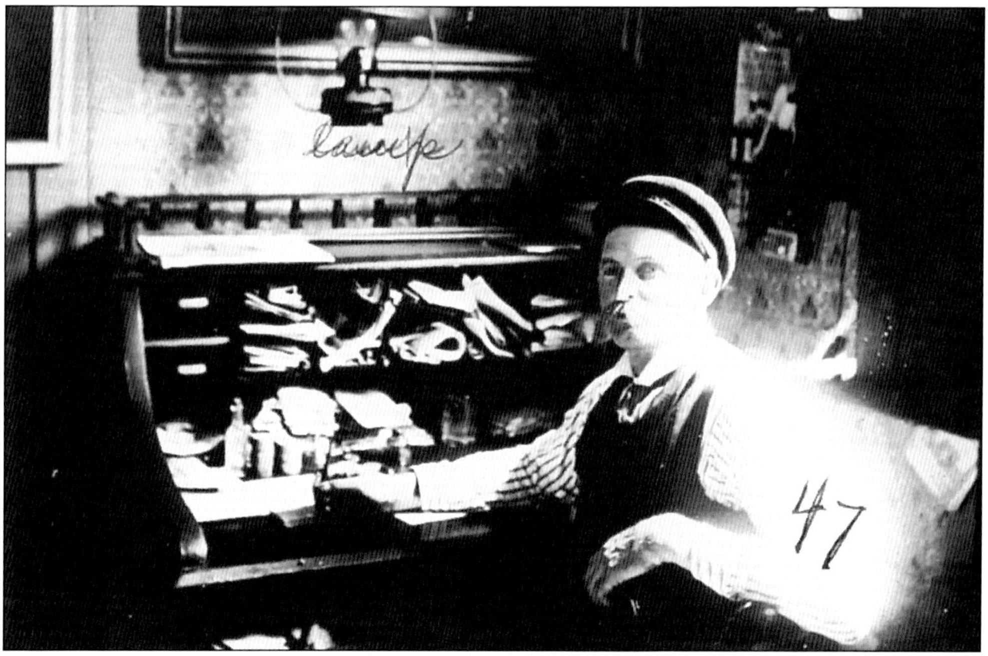

A rare interior view of the original post office around 1905, showing Postmaster Ralph G. Collins at his desk.

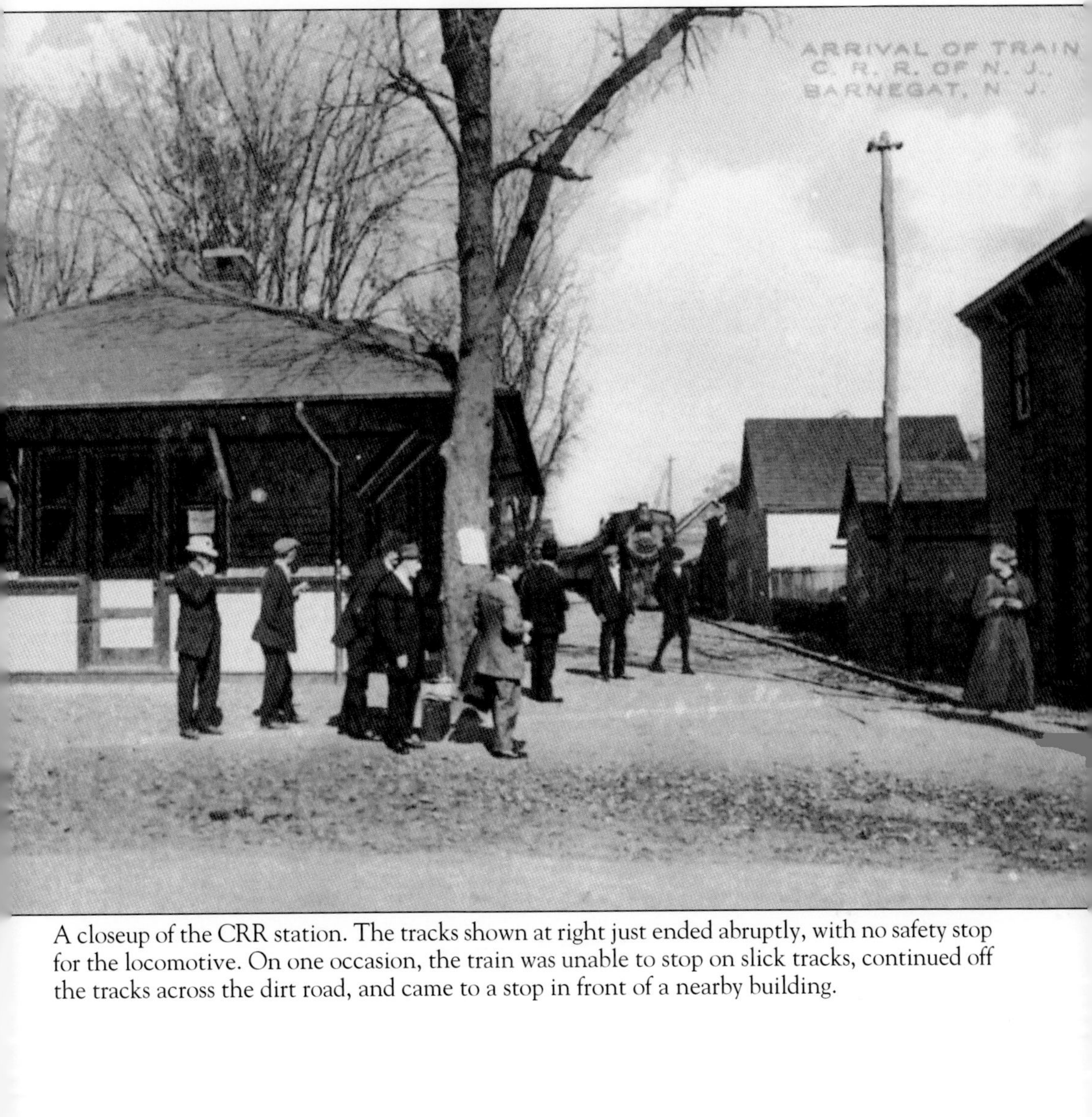

A closeup of the CRR station. The tracks shown at right just ended abruptly, with no safety stop for the locomotive. On one occasion, the train was unable to stop on slick tracks, continued off the tracks across the dirt road, and came to a stop in front of a nearby building.

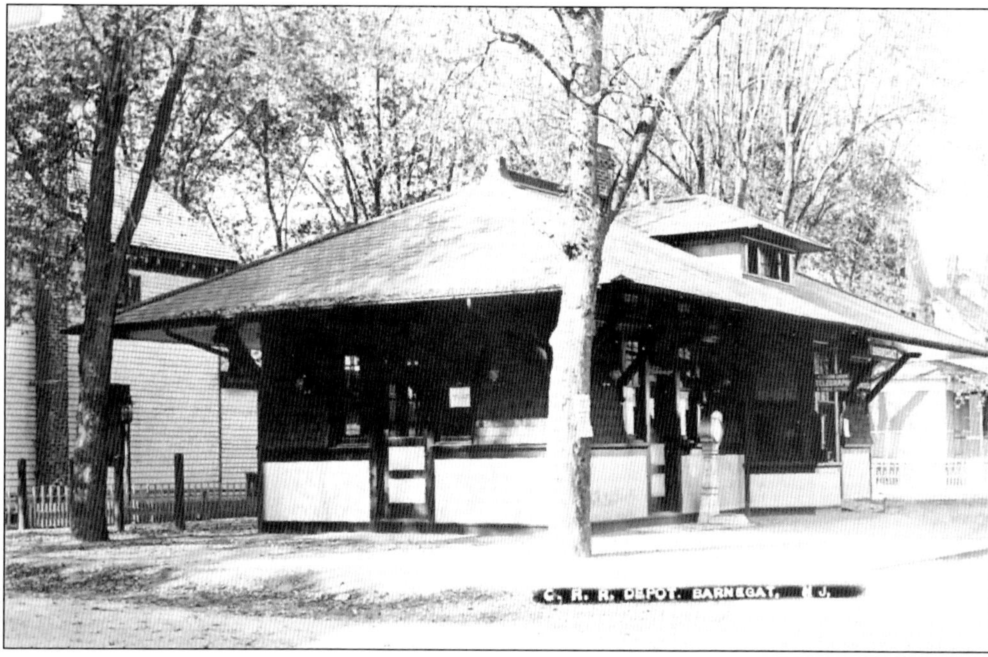

Another view of the Central Railroad station, this one taken in 1911. The station provided needed transportation to points north, and also served as the telegraph station. Take note of the penny scale on the platform.

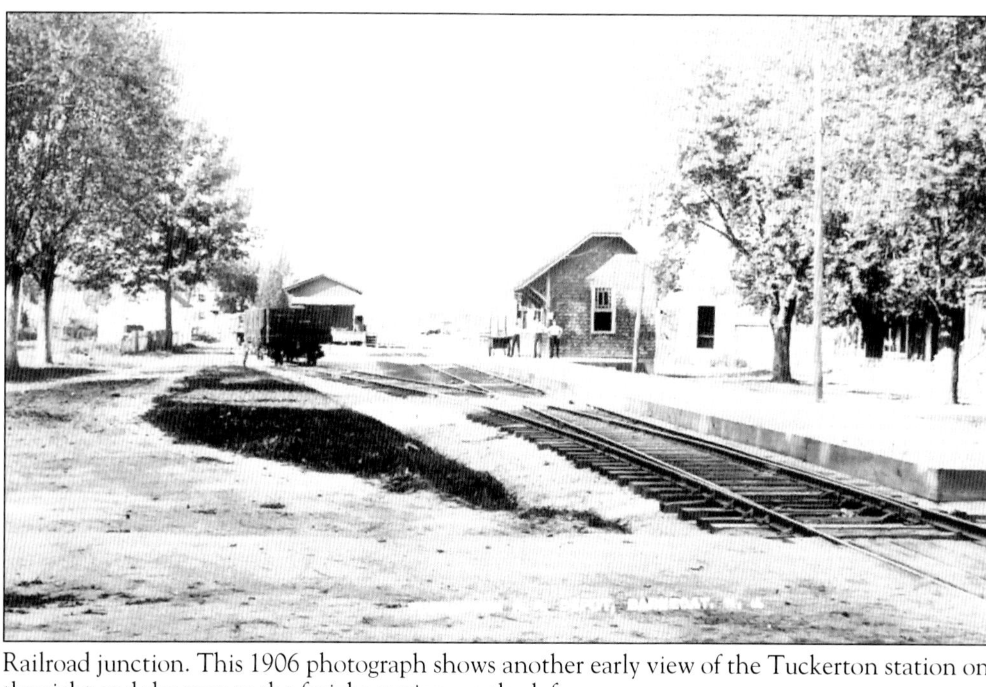

Railroad junction. This 1906 photograph shows another early view of the Tuckerton station on the right and the spur to the freight station on the left.

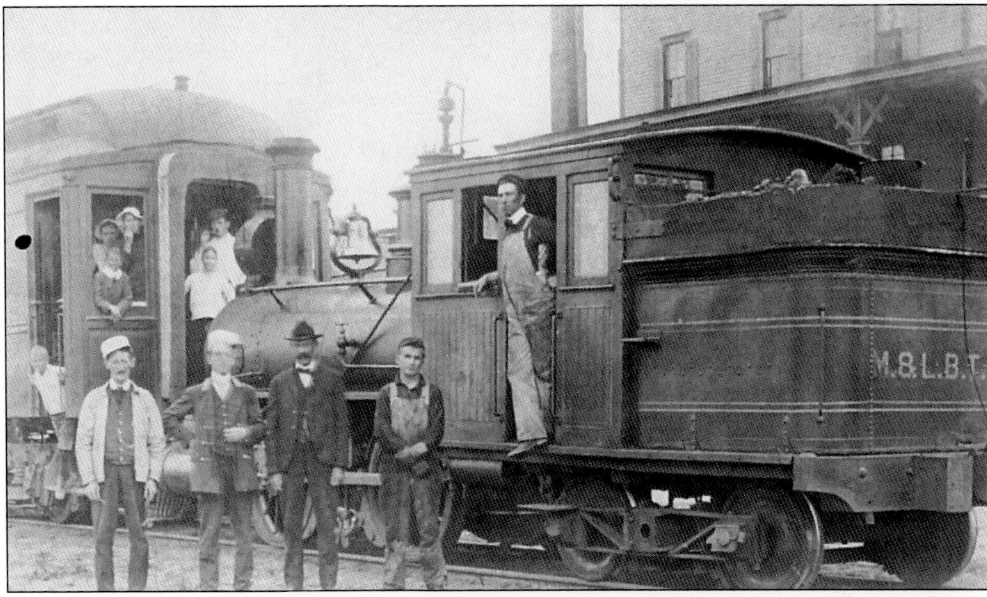

A passenger line. The Manahawkin and Long Beach Transportation Company operated on Long Beach Island from 1894 until its dissolution in 1909. This line shuttled passengers on its route from Manahawkin to Barnegat City.

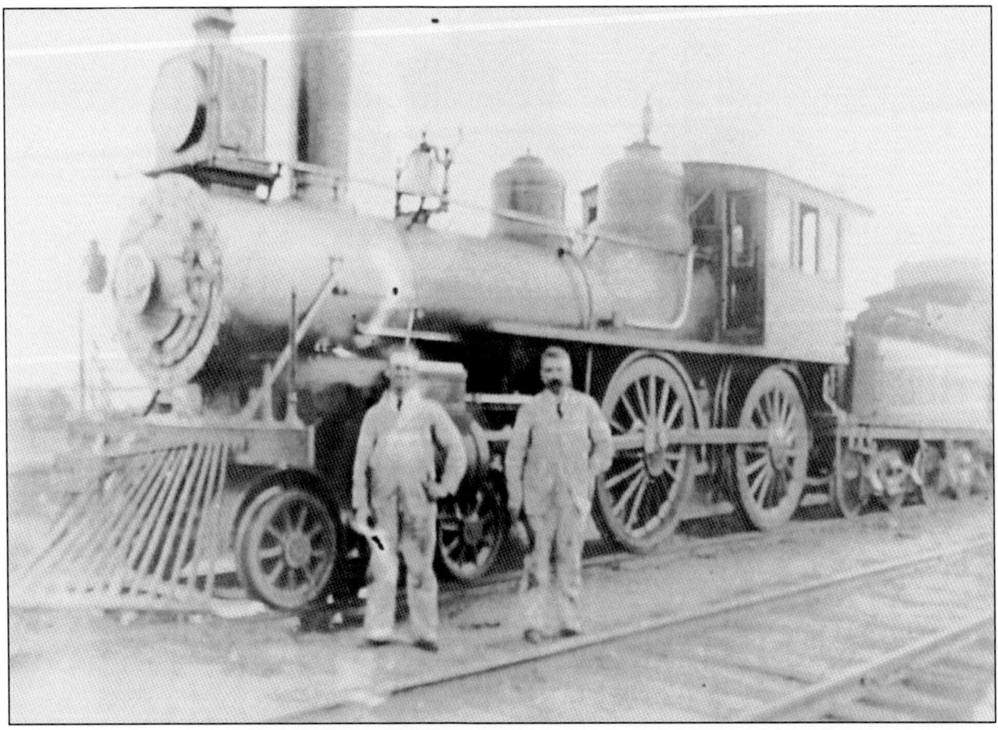

Central Railroad locomotive, photographed at Barnegat around 1905. The Ocean County area had an extensive network of train lines operating simultaneously. Today, only the northernmost part of the county has any train service at all.

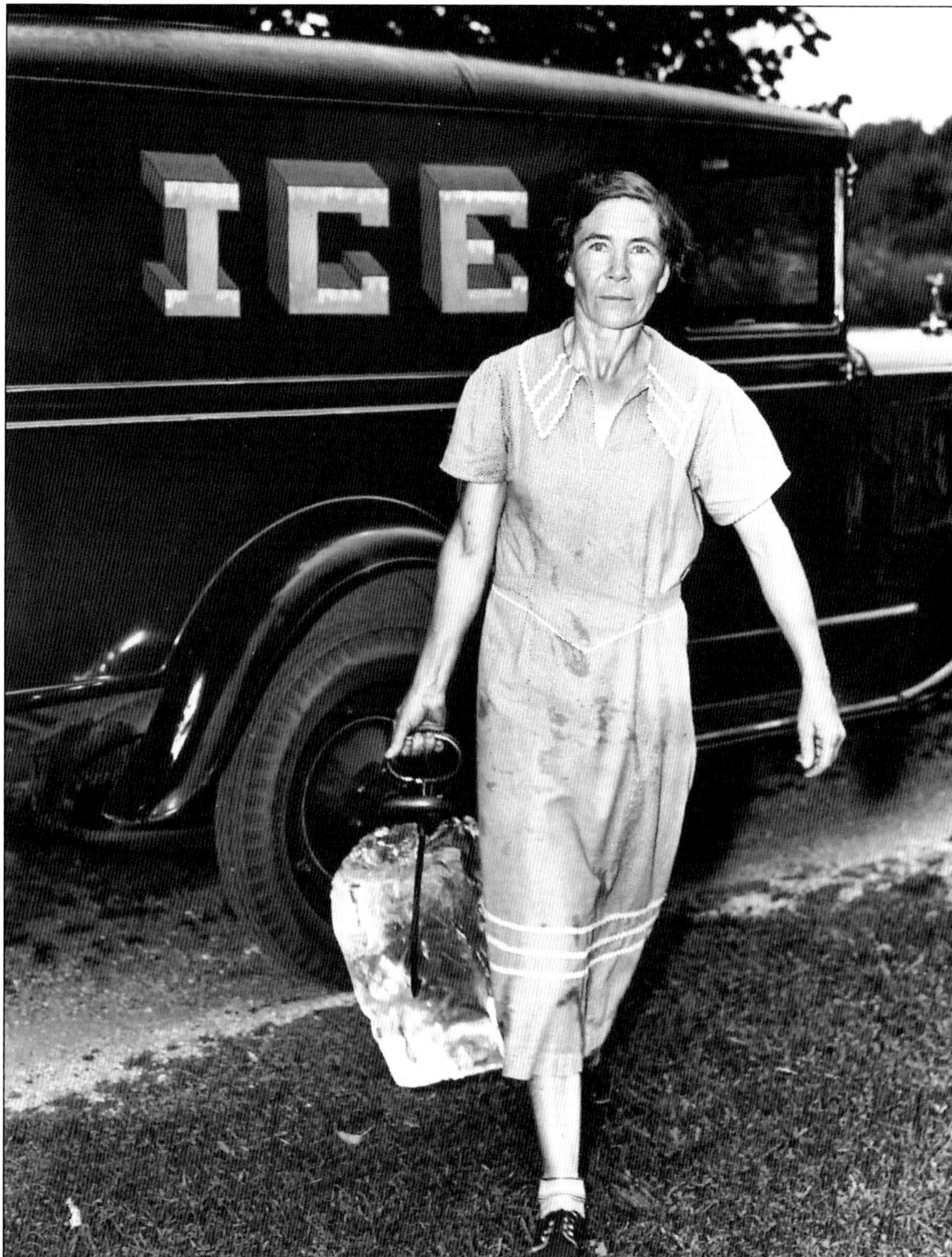

Mrs. Herbert, wife of the local Barnegat ice dealer. She often accompanied her husband, Theo Herbert, on his deliveries around town, and is shown here carrying a 50-pound block of ice.

Three

Business as Usual

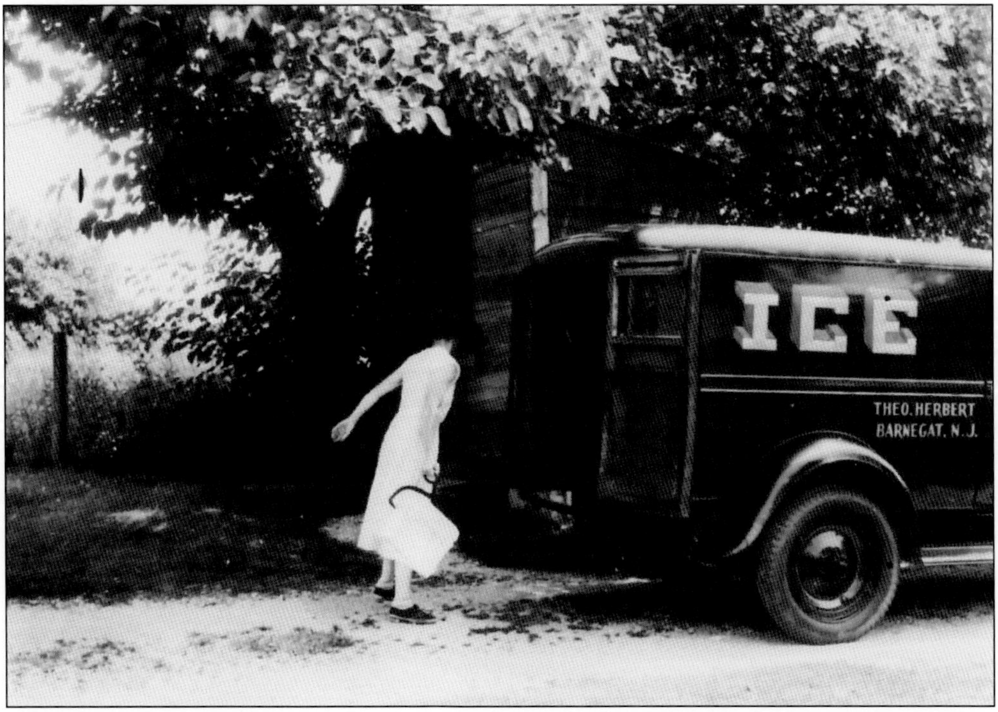

A common sight. Herbert's ice truck operated regularly around Barnegat in the 1920s and '30s. Ice was cut and stored during the winter months to be used in metal-lined ice boxes throughout the year.

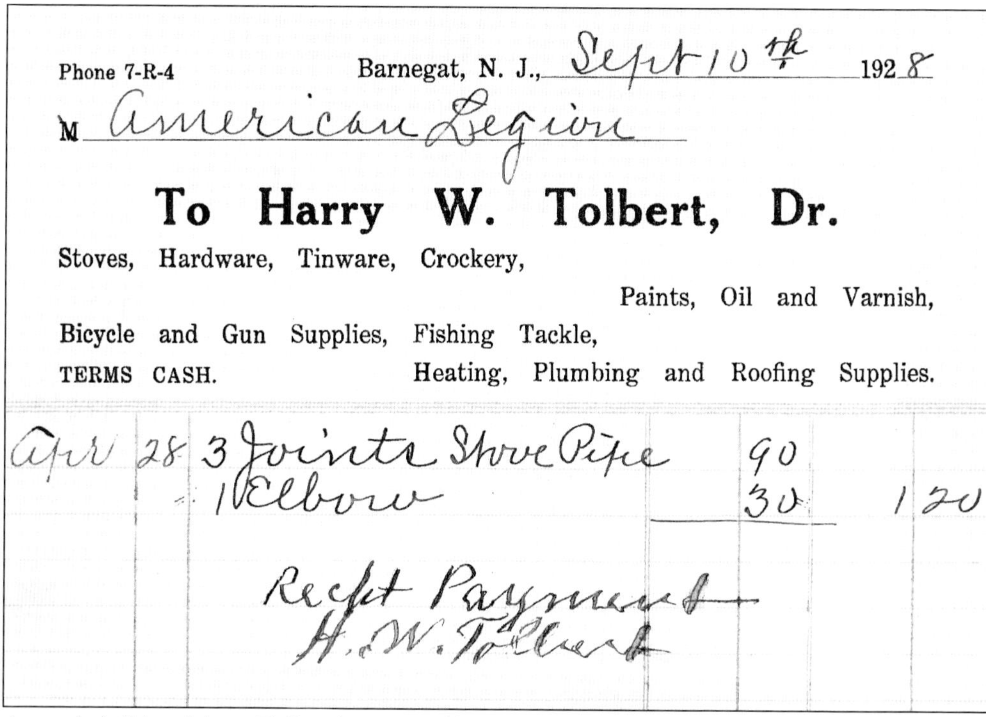

Phone 7-R-4 Barnegat, N. J., Sept 10th 1928

M American Legion

To Harry W. Tolbert, Dr.

Stoves, Hardware, Tinware, Crockery, Paints, Oil and Varnish,

Bicycle and Gun Supplies, Fishing Tackle,

TERMS CASH. Heating, Plumbing and Roofing Supplies.

Apr	28	3 Joints Stove Pipe	90	
		1 Elbow	30	1 20

Recd Payment

H. W. Tolbert

An early bill head from Tolbert's store in Barnegat. Harry Tolbert was a dealer in all types of hardware, as seen above. His store was located on the south side of East Bay Avenue.

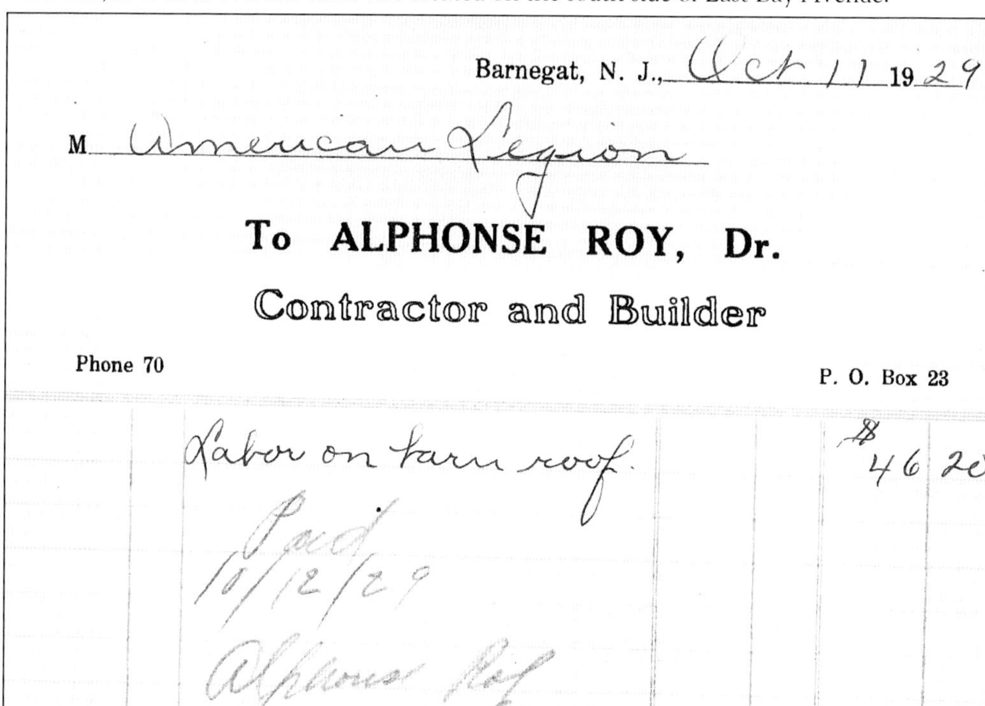

Barnegat, N. J., Oct 11 1929

M American Legion

To ALPHONSE ROY, Dr.

Contractor and Builder

Phone 70 P. O. Box 23

Labor on barn roof.	$46 20

Paid

10/12/29

Alphonse Roy

Bill head from a builder of many local homes and commercial buildings. Many residences were built from recycled lumber that was washed ashore from the shipwrecks on Long Beach Island.

"Silkworm Charlie's." This well-known business was family owned and operated and flourished around 1910. Several buildings were devoted to the industry, one for the raising and formation of cocoons, another for the feeding of silkworms, and yet another for the processing of silk. The operation was located on the west side of South Main Street (Route 9).

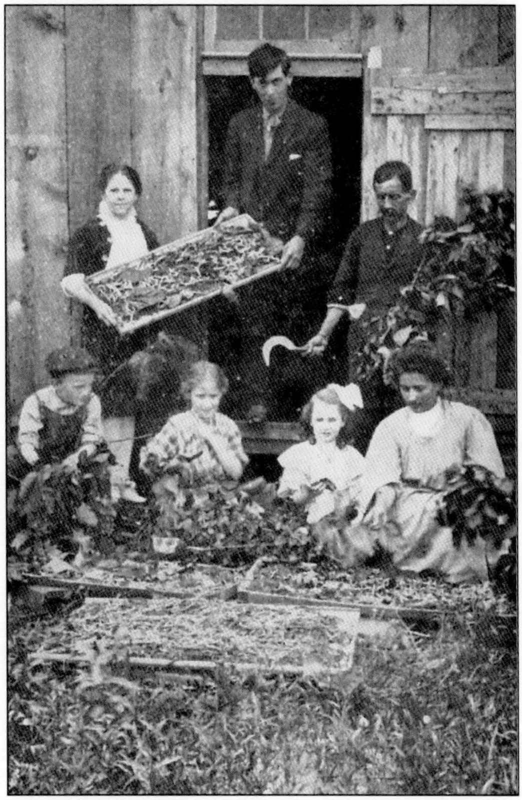

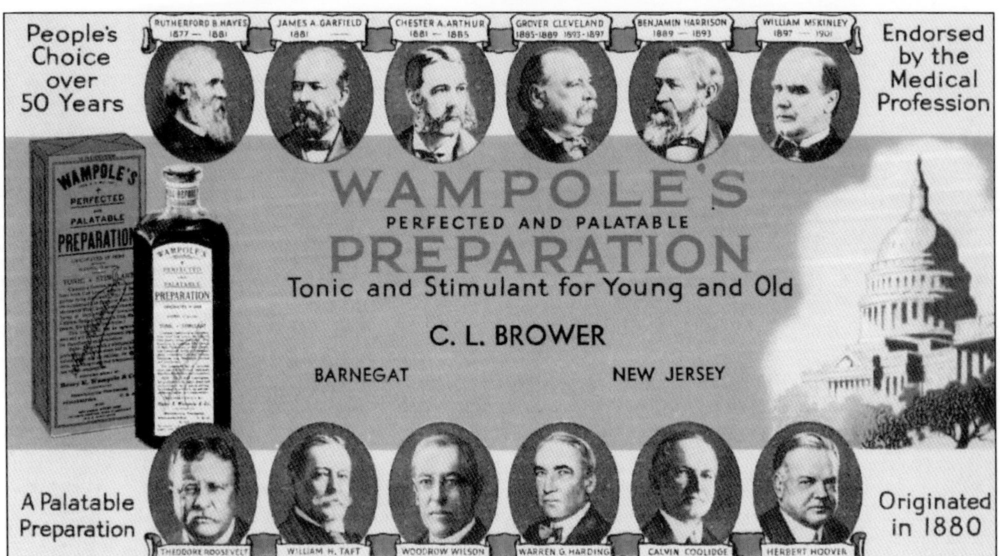

An early giveaway blotter for C.L. Browers drugstore. It advertises "Wampoles Perfected and Palatable Preparation." Area businesses always had giveaways printed to advertise and entice consumers to buy their products.

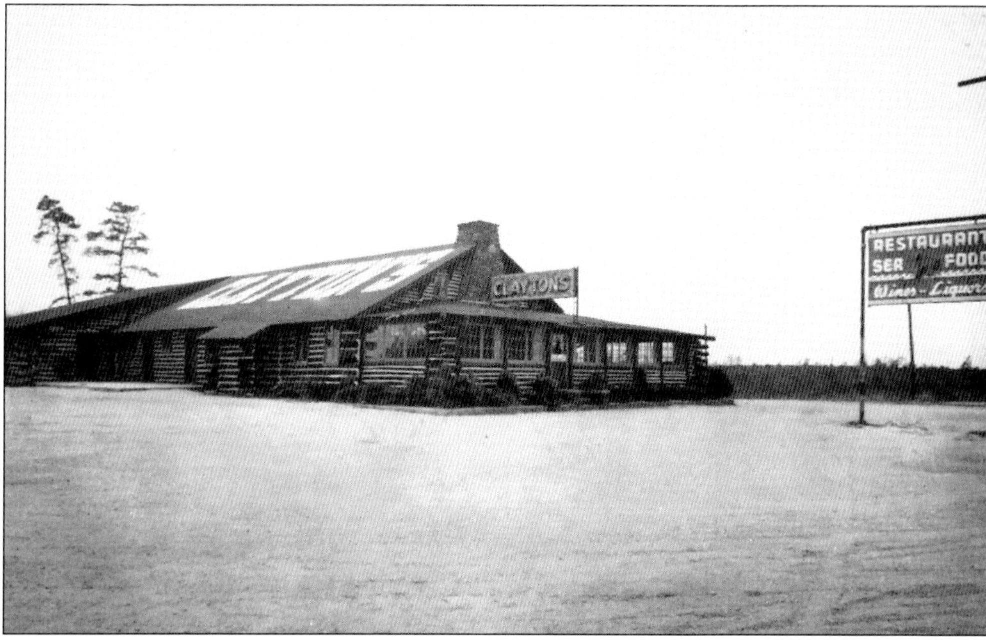

A 1936 view of Clayton's Log Cabin Restaurant on old Route 5-40 (now Route 72). This highway was also known as the Philadelphia/Beach Haven Highway. This building was built by Northrup Clayton of cedar gathered from a nearby swamp.

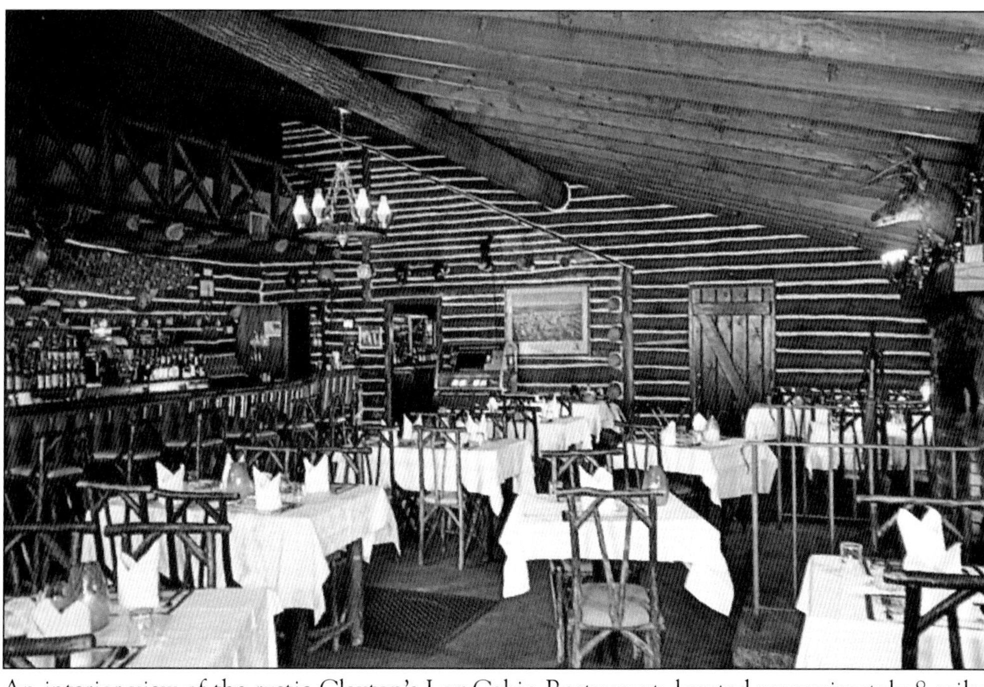

An interior view of the rustic Clayton's Log Cabin Restaurant, located approximately 8 miles west of Manahawkin. The restaurant took four years to build; construction lasted from 1932 until 1936. It still remains in business today.

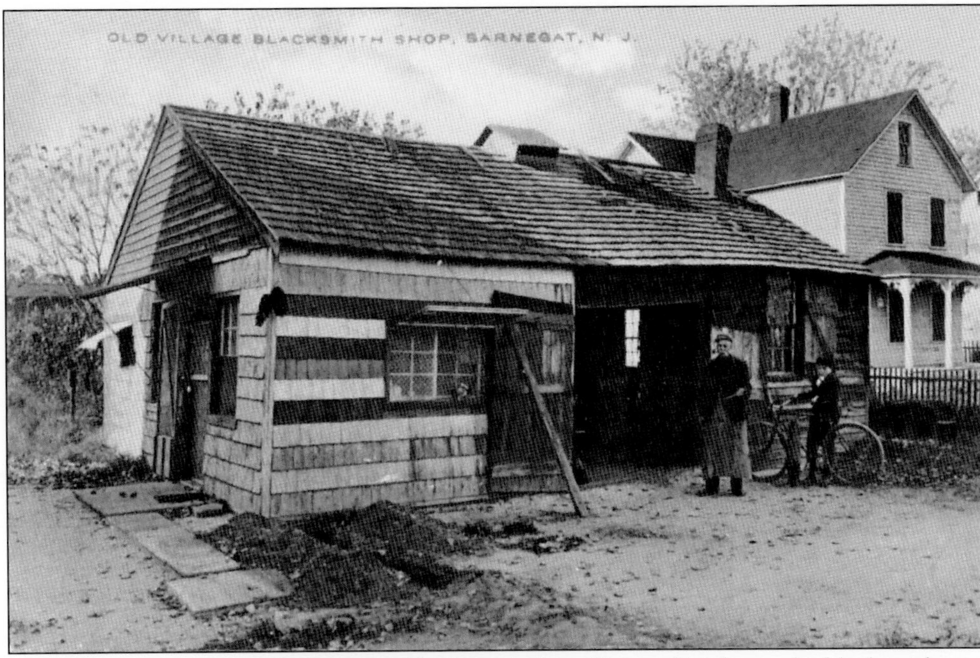

A 1914 postcard view of the Barnegat blacksmith shop. Horace Errickson, the blacksmith, was responsible for most of the early forged tools and hardware in town. The shop was located on the west side of North Main Street (Route 9).

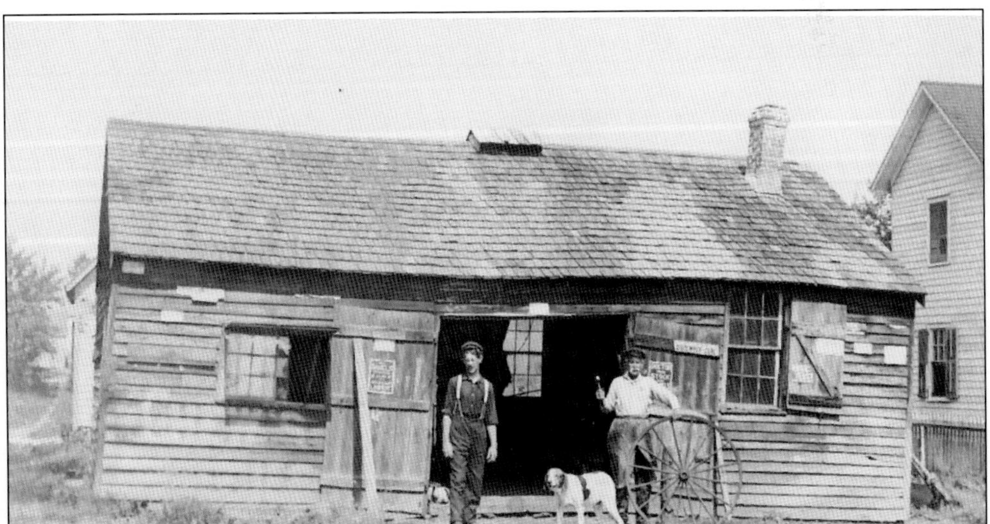

A 1909 real-photo postcard view of Errickson's blacksmith shop. Horace Errickson is shown at right with Harry (Pete) Ridgeway on his left. Note the many early advertising signs for "Dr. Daniels Veterinary Medicines," "Distemper Cure," "Magic Yeast," and "Doctor your Stock."

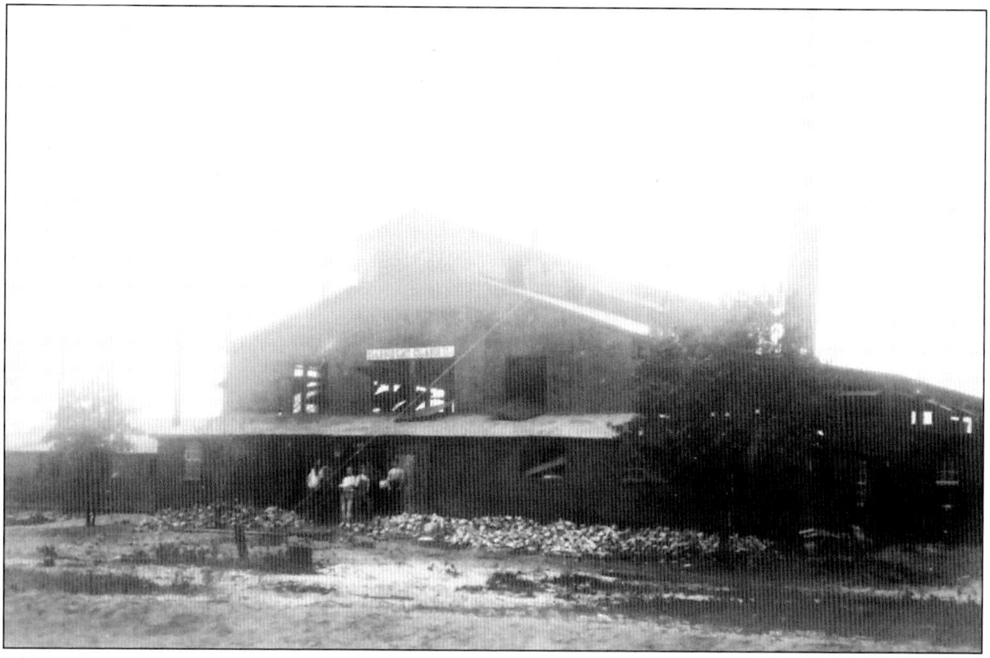

The Barnegat Glass Company, one of Barnegat's largest employers. Built in 1896, this factory produced glass of all kinds from the fine local sand. The factory was located on the west side of North Main Street (Route 9). Note the piles of broken glass or "cullet" stacked out front, ready to be re-melted. The glass company is shown here c. 1910

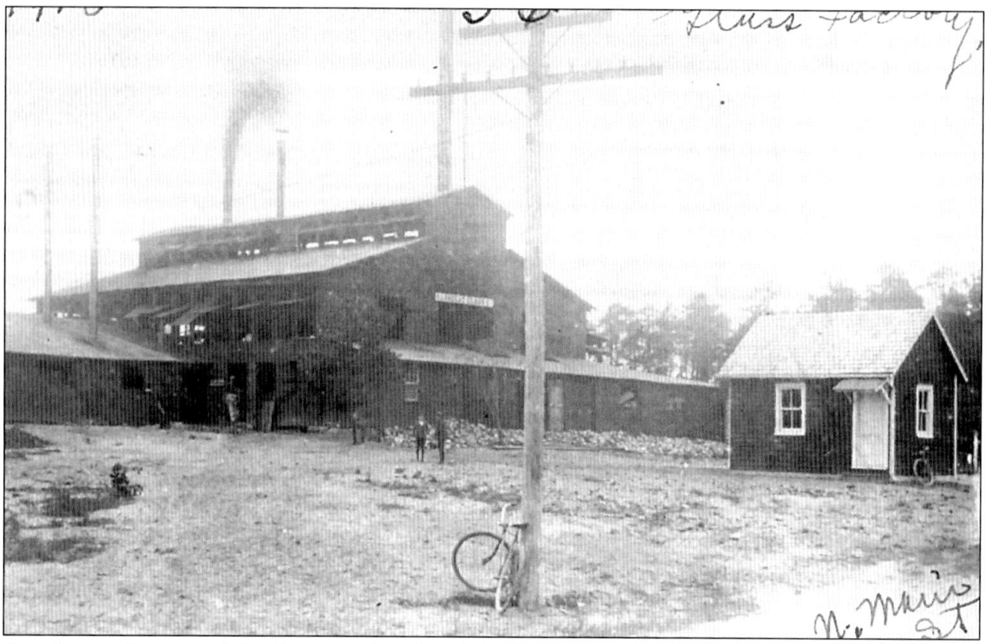

Another early view of the factory taken from North Main Street. The company employed many men and boys as young as eight years old to man the furnaces and blow pipes. Production continued until 1914. A fire later destroyed the building.

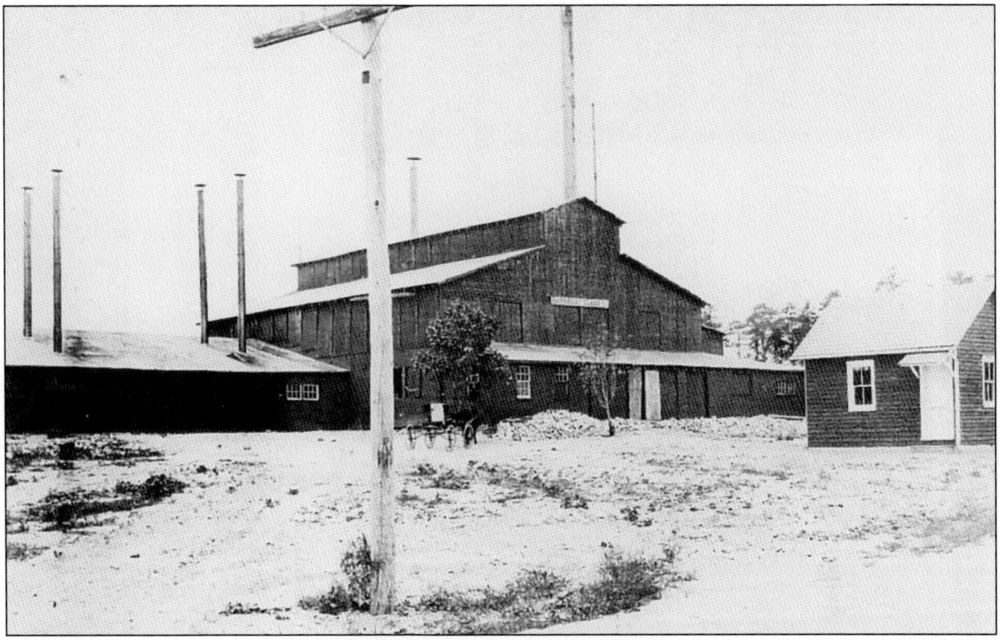

A historic enterprise. Begun as the Barnegat Druggist Holloware Company many years earlier, the Barnegat Glass Company underwent several ownership changes through the years. Its demise came around 1914 when glassware and bottles came to be manufactured mostly by machine.

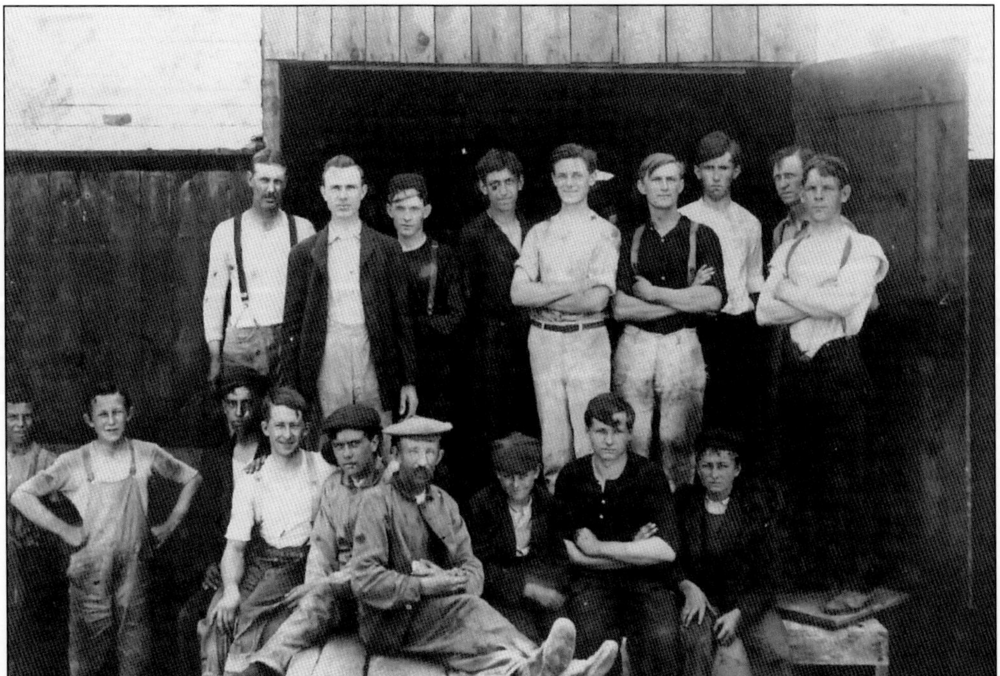

The glassworks crew at Barnegat *c.* 1908. Note the young age of some of the workers. Temperatures in the factory often topped 100 degrees!

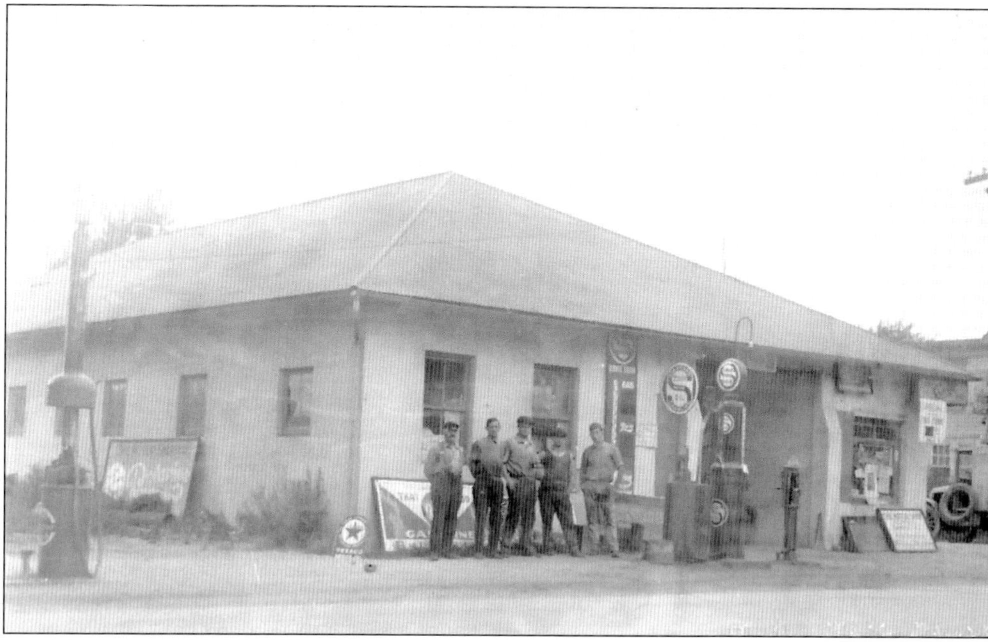

Gaskills' Garage and Motor Shop c. 1920. The shop was located on the west side of South Main Street at West Brook Street. Owned by Sam Gaskill and his father Joseph Gaskill, the shop serviced all types of automobiles and equipment. Note the early glass-topped gas pumps out front.

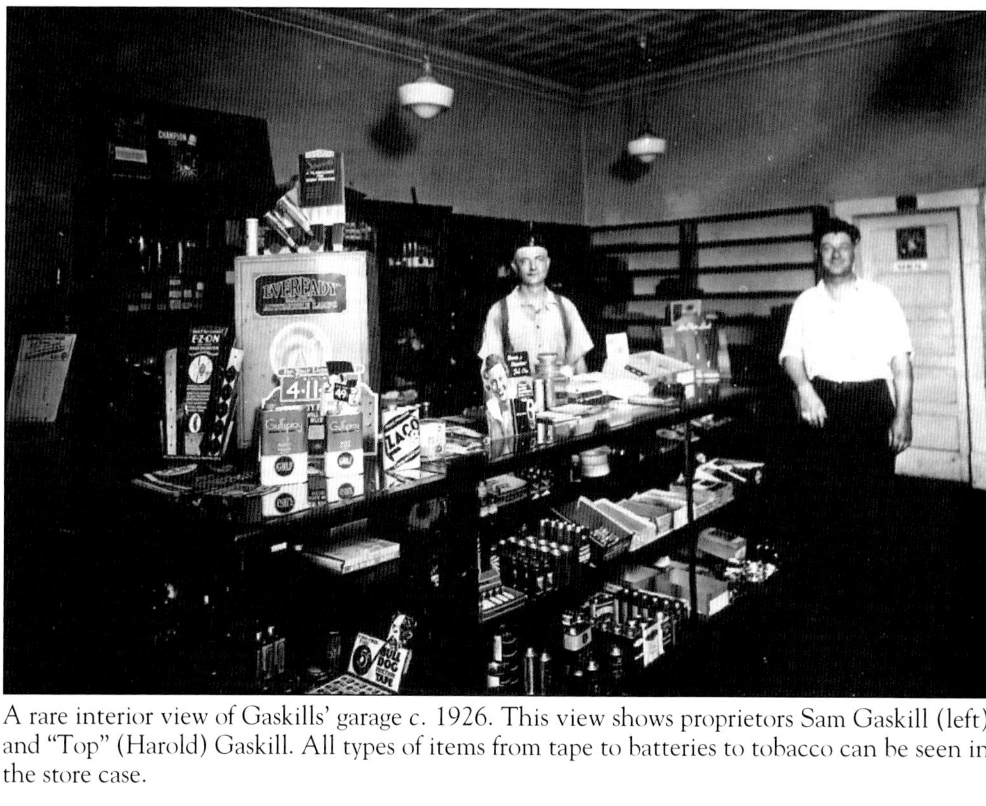

A rare interior view of Gaskills' garage c. 1926. This view shows proprietors Sam Gaskill (left) and "Top" (Harold) Gaskill. All types of items from tape to batteries to tobacco can be seen in the store case.

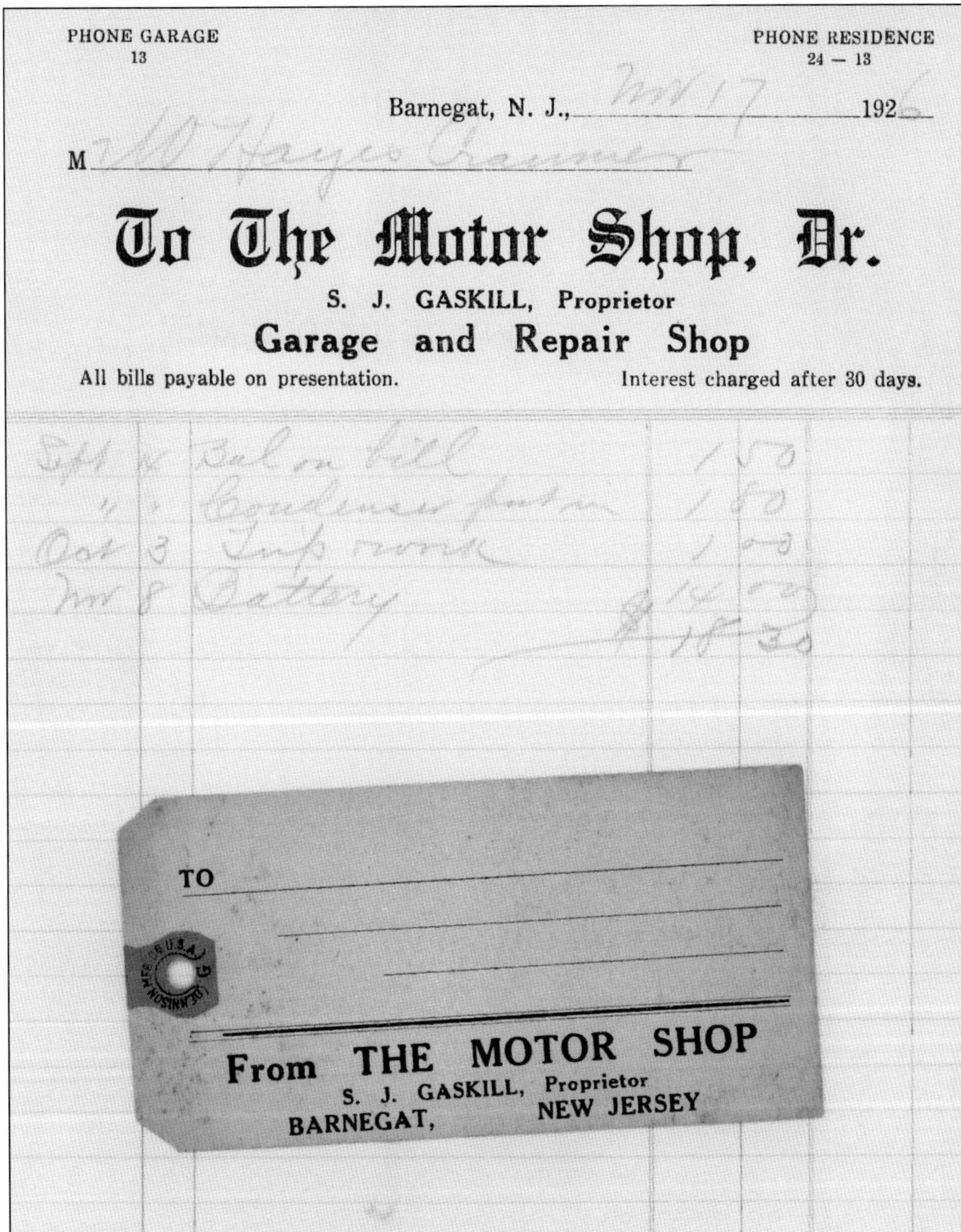

A 1920s bill head and motor tag from Gaskills' garage on South Main Street. This building still stands today.

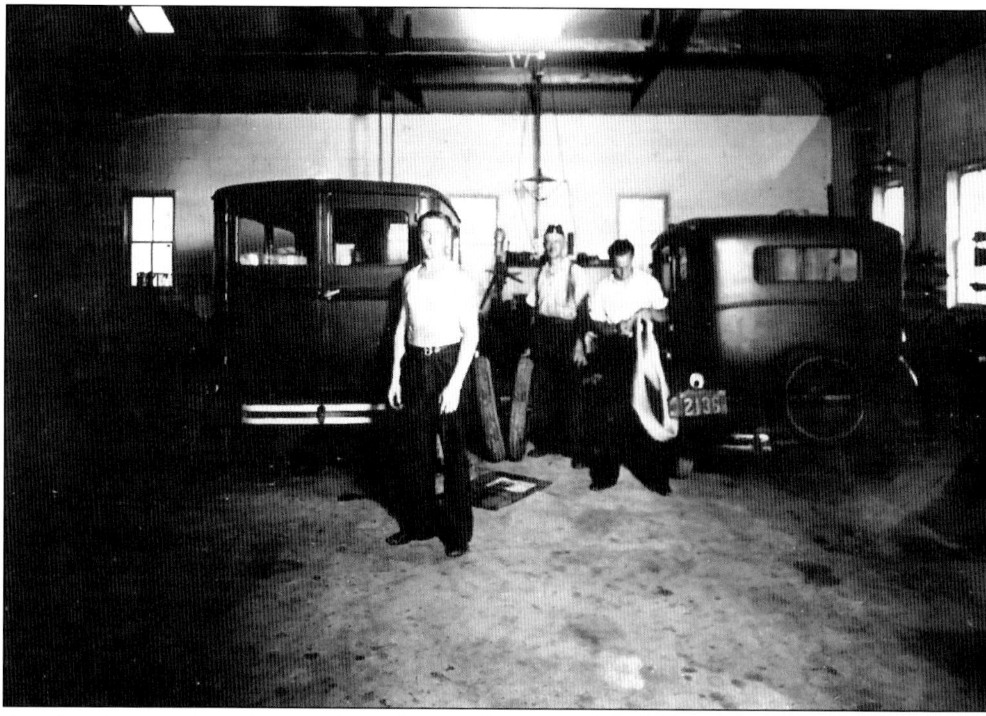

Another interior view, this one from the auto bay area of Gaskills' garage c. 1925.

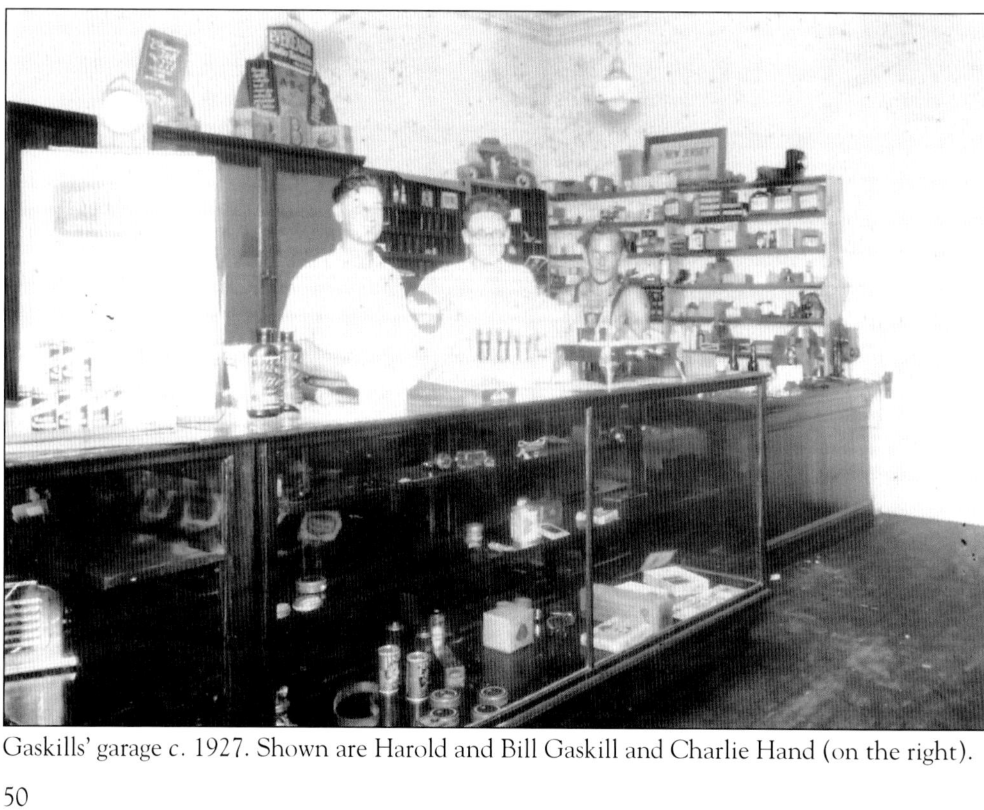

Gaskills' garage c. 1927. Shown are Harold and Bill Gaskill and Charlie Hand (on the right).

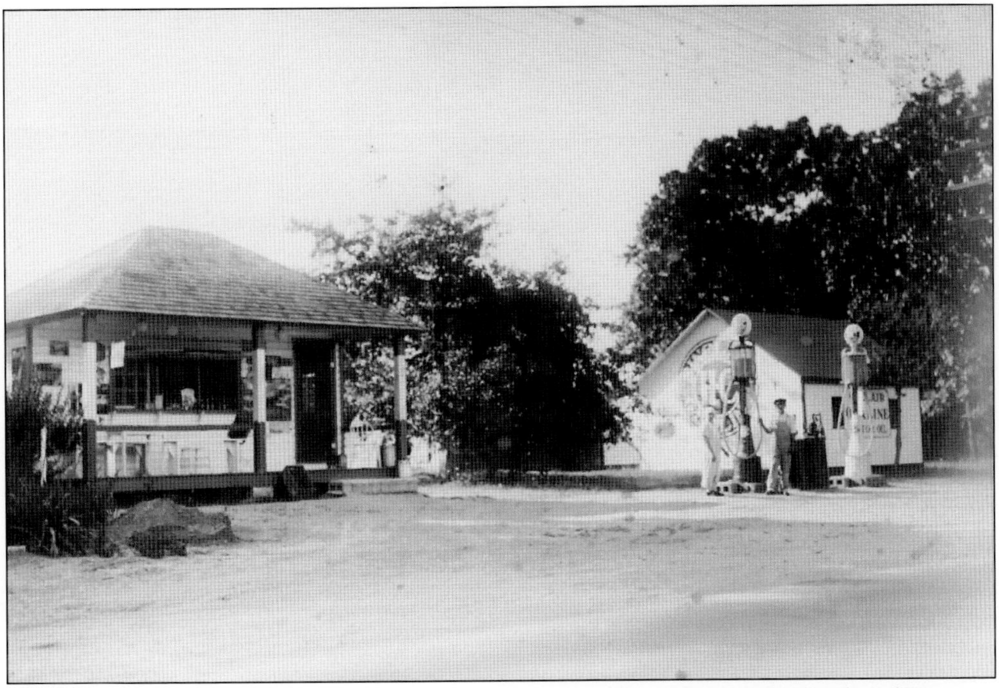

Early gas station. This service station stood south of Gaskills' garage on the border of Barnegat and Manahawkin. It specialized in Sinclair fuel and even had a snack shop on the premises.

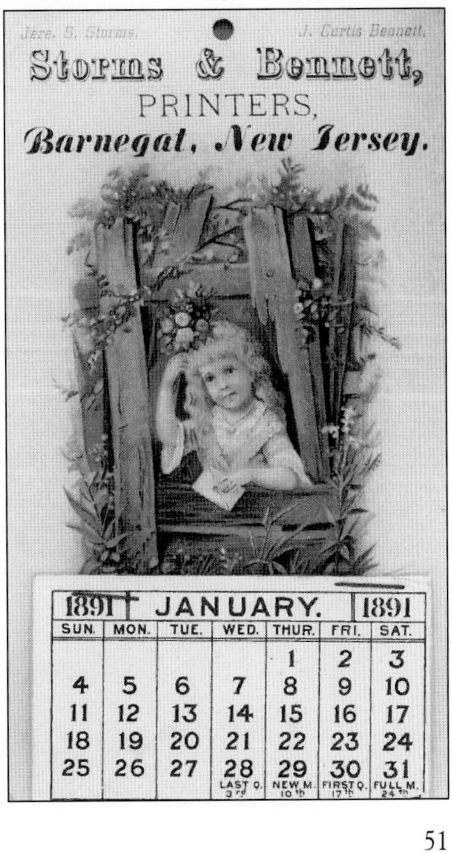

A very early advertising calendar for Storms and Bennett, Printers. The company was responsible for most of the printed advertising and literature of this time in the area.

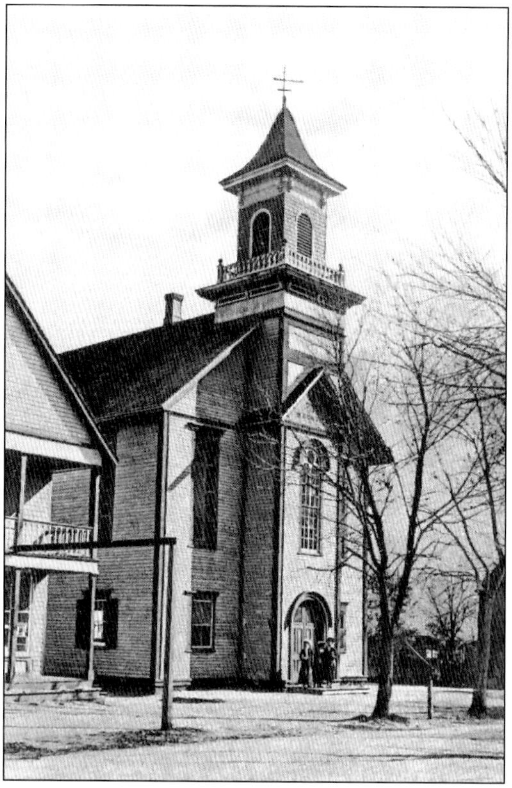

Barnegat Methodist Church c. 1910. Built in 1882, it replaced an earlier church that burned the same year. The church was and still is located on the corner of East Bay Avenue and Birdsall Street.

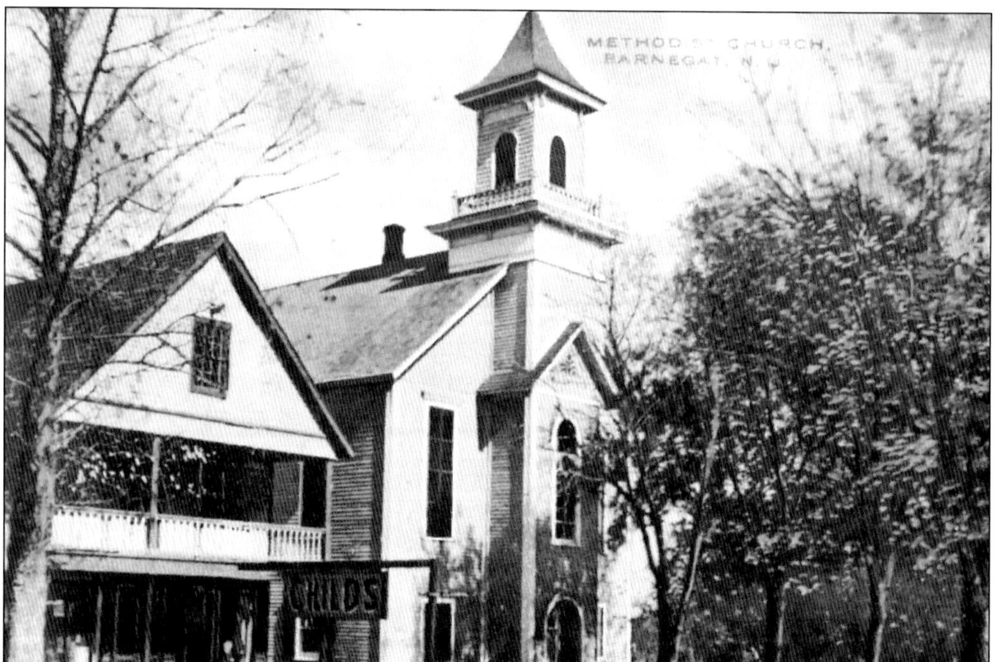

Another view of the Methodist church, this one c. 1910. Note the height of the church steeple, which replaced a taller, earlier version.

Four

Church and School

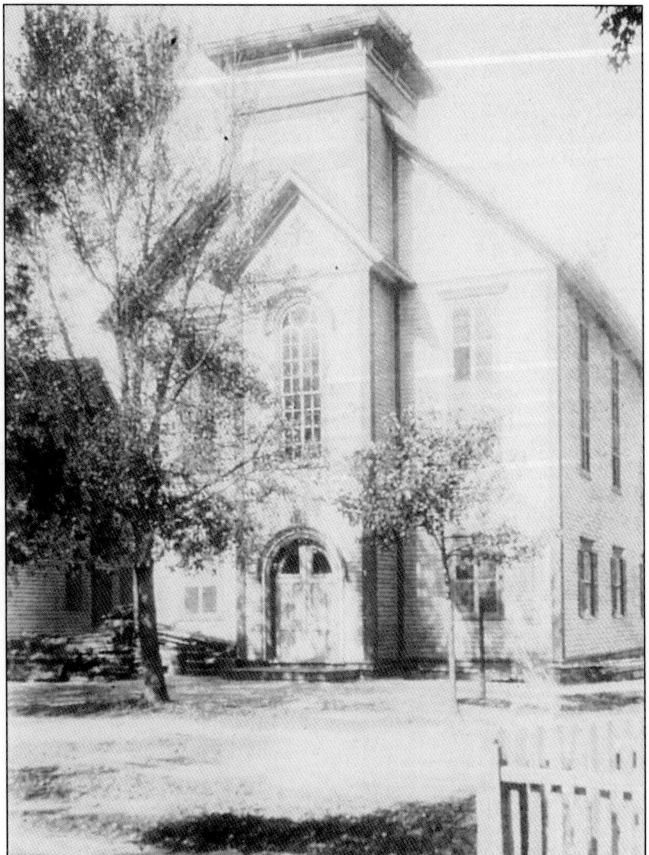

A c. 1903 view of the Methodist church. The tall church steeple had been destroyed in a terrible storm.

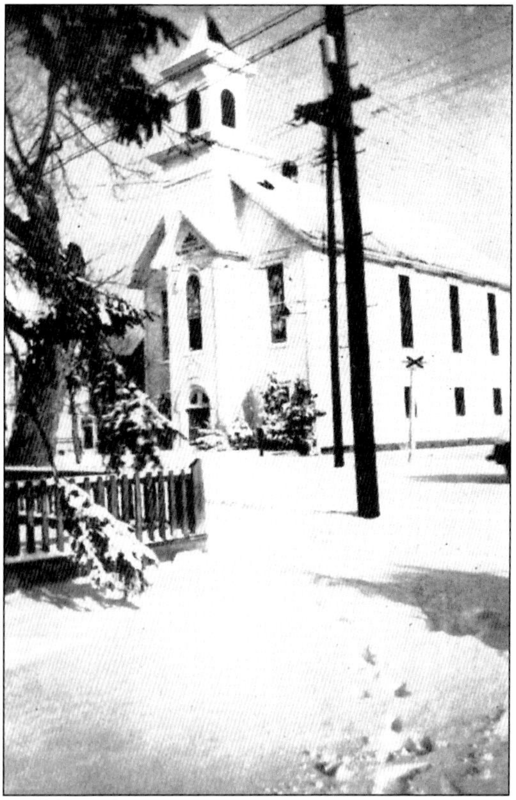

A view of the Barnegat Methodist Church as it appears today.

Sacrificed to the storm. In a terrible gale on September 16, 1903, the tall steeple tumbled off the roof of the Methodist church and crashed through the building next door. A clerk from the store left for home minutes before the disaster. No one was hurt.

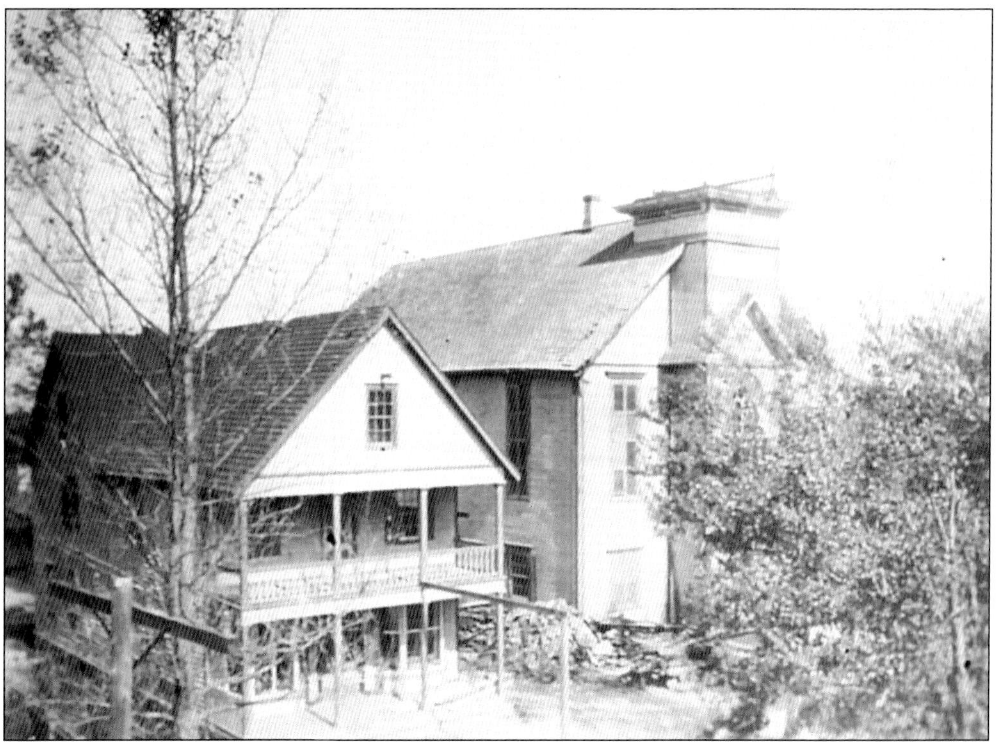

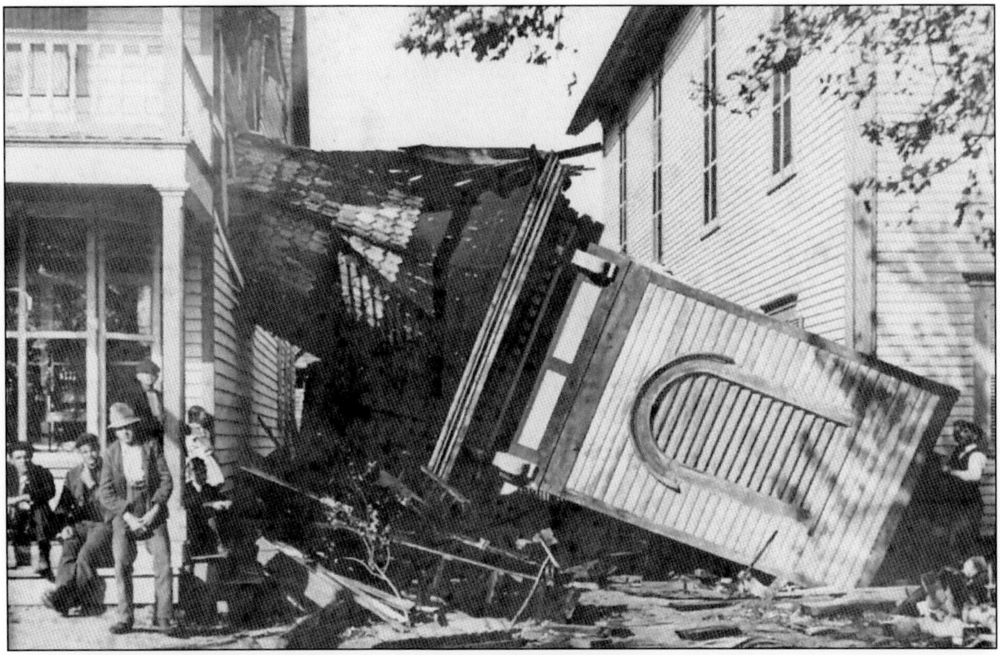

An unbelievable sight. People came out from all over town to see the steeple disaster. Plans were made to replace the same steeple, but organizers later decided to utilize a smaller, shorter design.

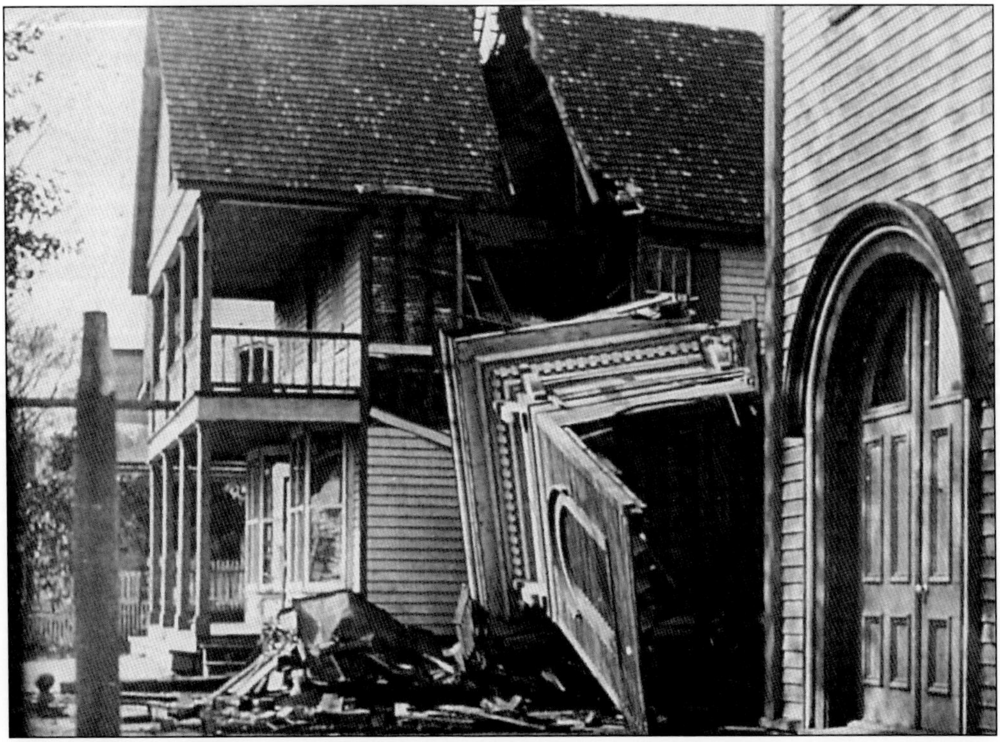

Damage control. Both the church steeple and the store next door were repaired within weeks. This picture was taken in September 1903.

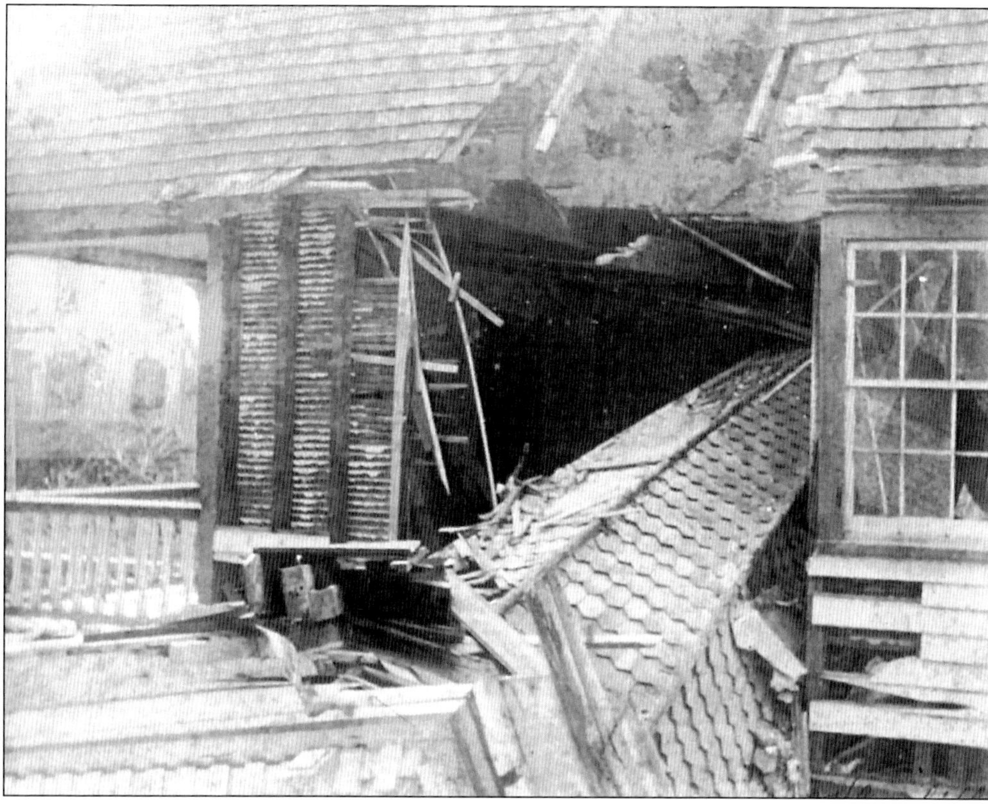

Another disaster view showing the heavy damage caused by the fallen steeple.

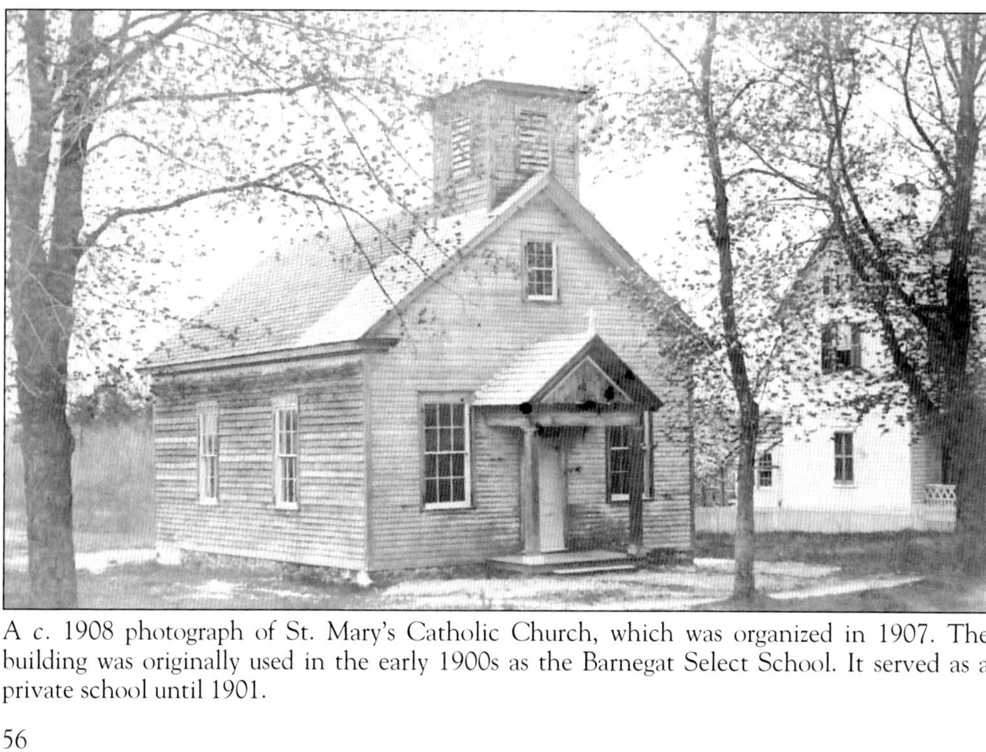

A c. 1908 photograph of St. Mary's Catholic Church, which was organized in 1907. The building was originally used in the early 1900s as the Barnegat Select School. It served as a private school until 1901.

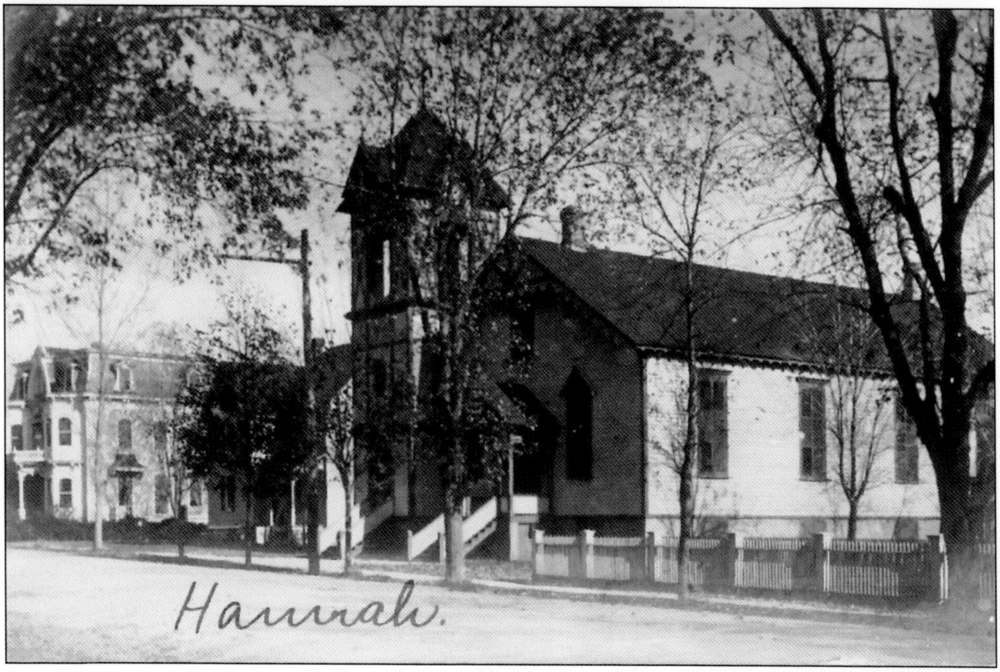

A 1905 view of the Presbyterian church on South Main Street (Route 9). Built before 1876, this building originally served as an opera house; it was converted to a church in 1876.

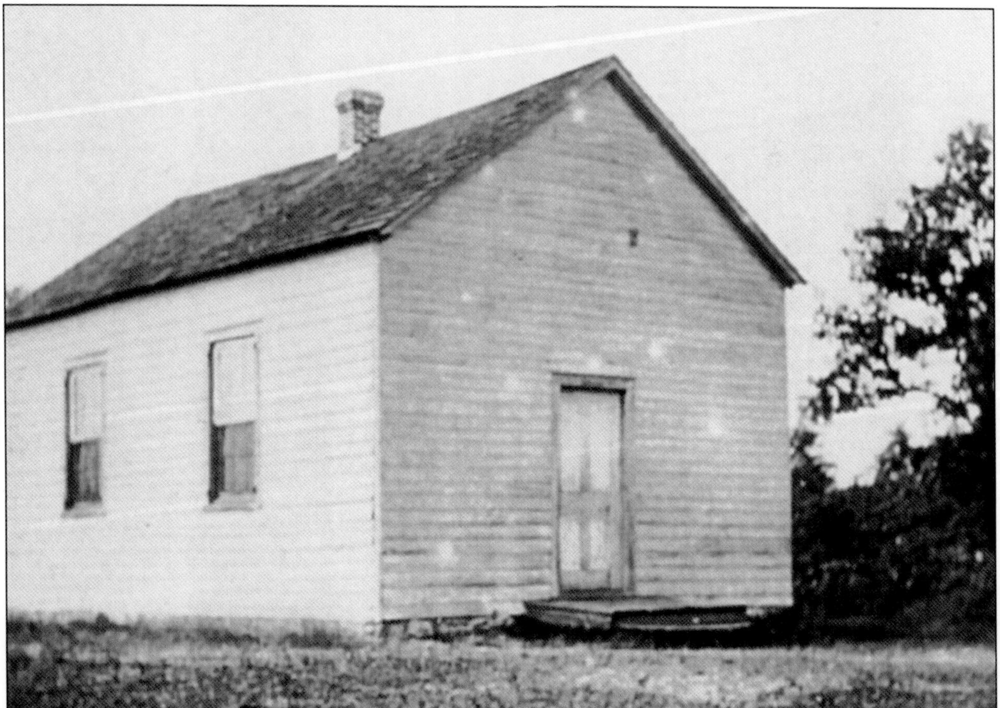

An early view of the Brookville church on the western border of Barnegat Township. Although a town in itself—complete with a school, church, and general store—Brookville is often considered to be part of Barnegat.

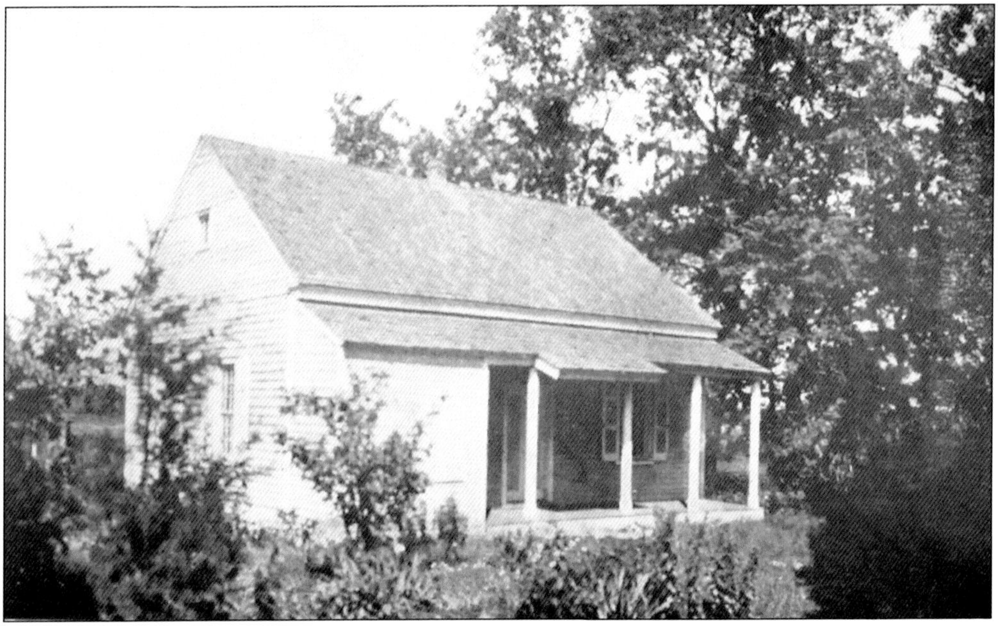

The Quaker Meeting House. One of the earliest churches in Barnegat, the Quaker Meeting House was built in 1767. This was the first known church in Barnegat, and only the third church building in all of Ocean County.

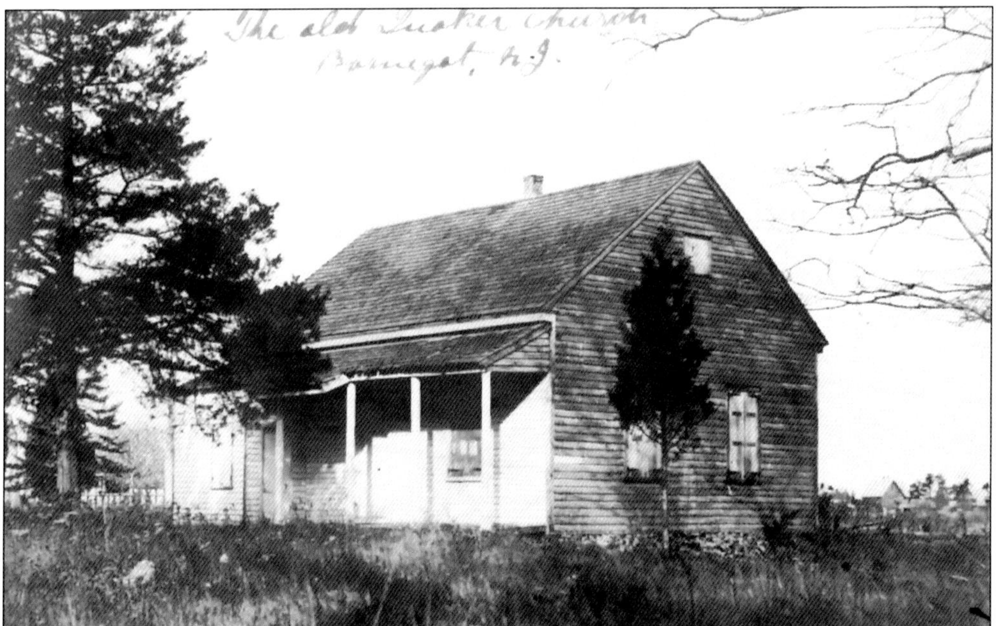

The Quaker Meeting House, 1909. The meetinghouse was located on the north side of East Bay Avenue. Its cemetery is marked with tombstones dating back over 170 years, many of which belong to victims of early local shipwrecks.

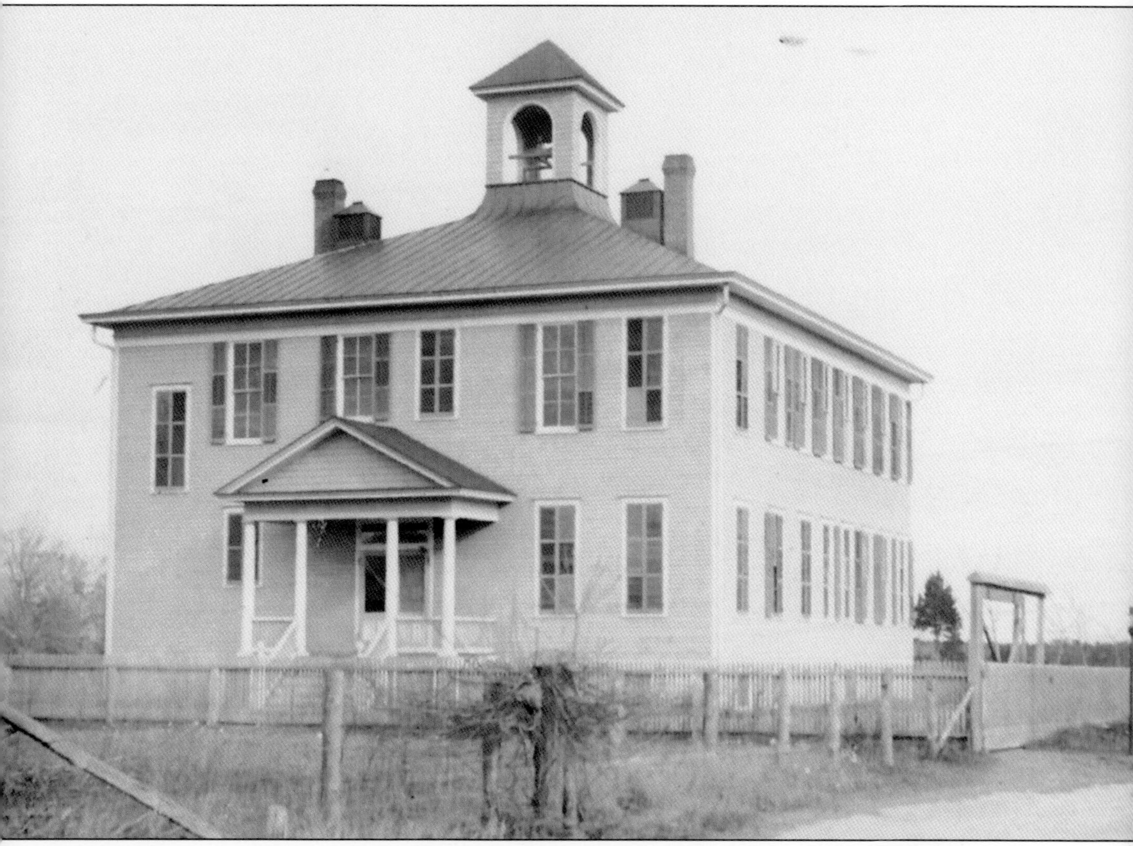

A 1910 view of the Barnegat Public School. Used as a grade school from 1901 until 1957, it was razed in 1962. It was also used as a high school for a period of time. This view looks north.

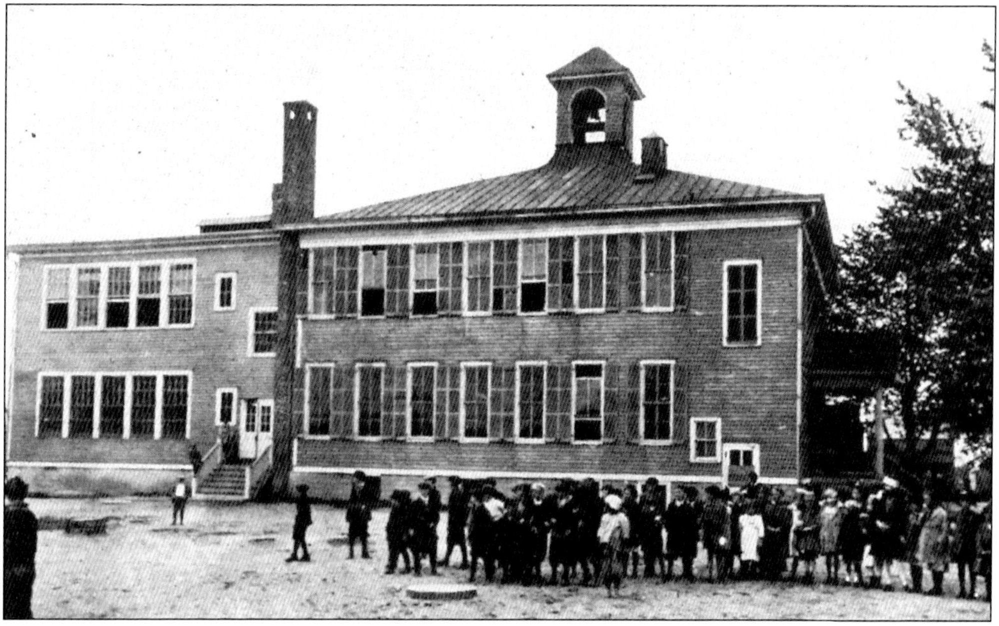

A c. 1923 view of the public school. Note the addition to the main building. The original school bell is in the collection of the Barnegat Heritage Center.

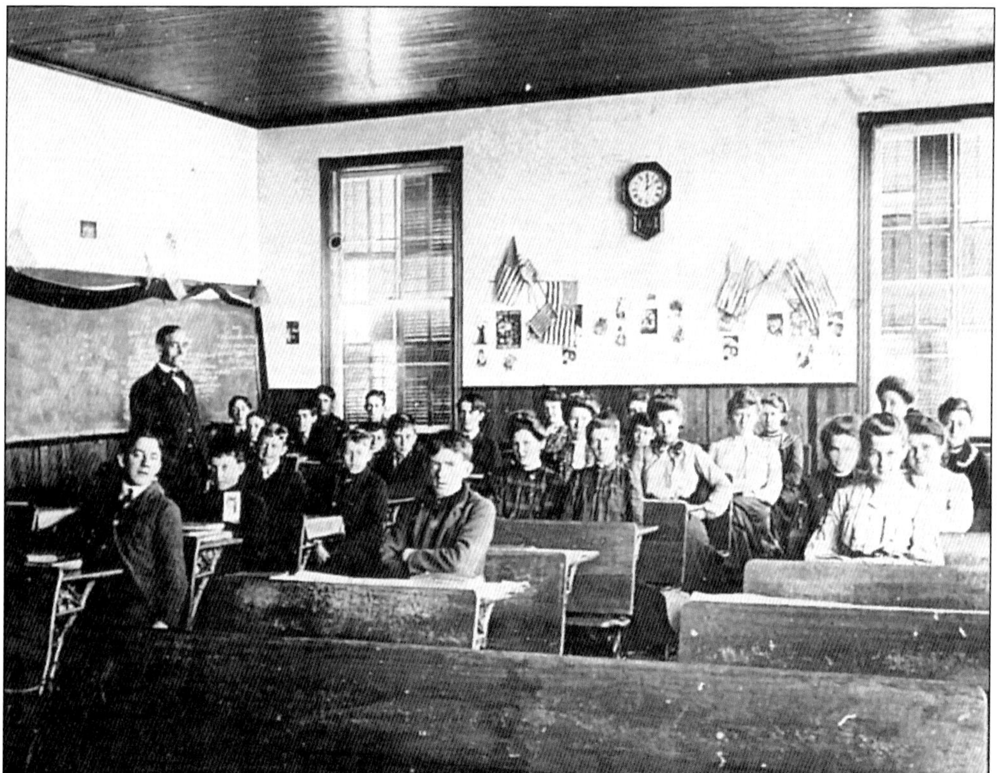

A c. 1905 interior view of the Barnegat Public School classroom. Note the old wooden shutters used to "ward off distractions," as the teachers used to say.

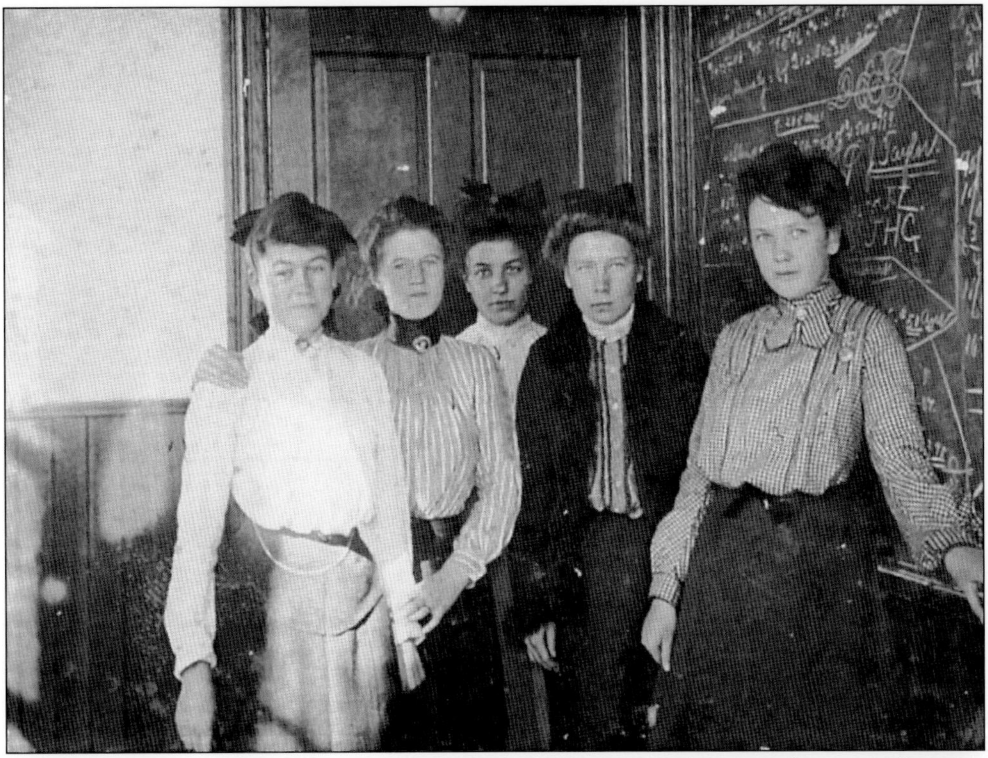

Another interior view of the Barnegat Public School classrooms, this one taken around 1910.

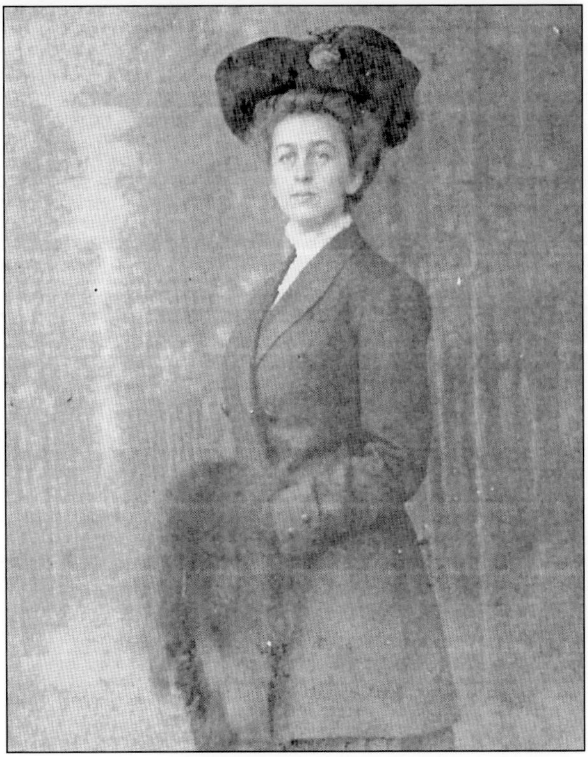

An early portrait of one of Barnegat's primary educators, Elizabeth V. Edwards, taken around 1910. Elizabeth was educated in Barnegat and began teaching at age twenty-five in 1901. She continued to teach until she retired in the 1940s. A local school was named in honor of her in 1983.

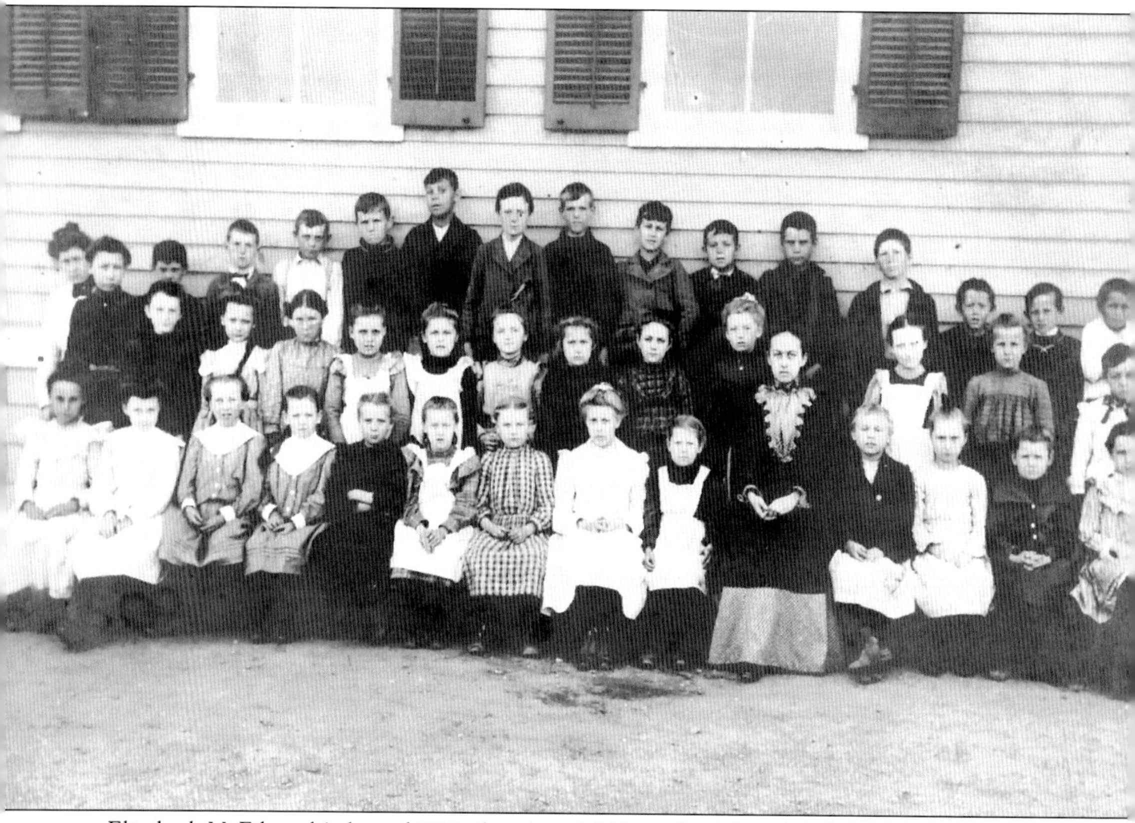

Elizabeth V. Edwards' class of 1901: fourth and fifth grades. Many local children shown bear the names of longtime Barnegat families: Inman, Predmore, Ridgeway, Birdsall, Soper, and Bahr.

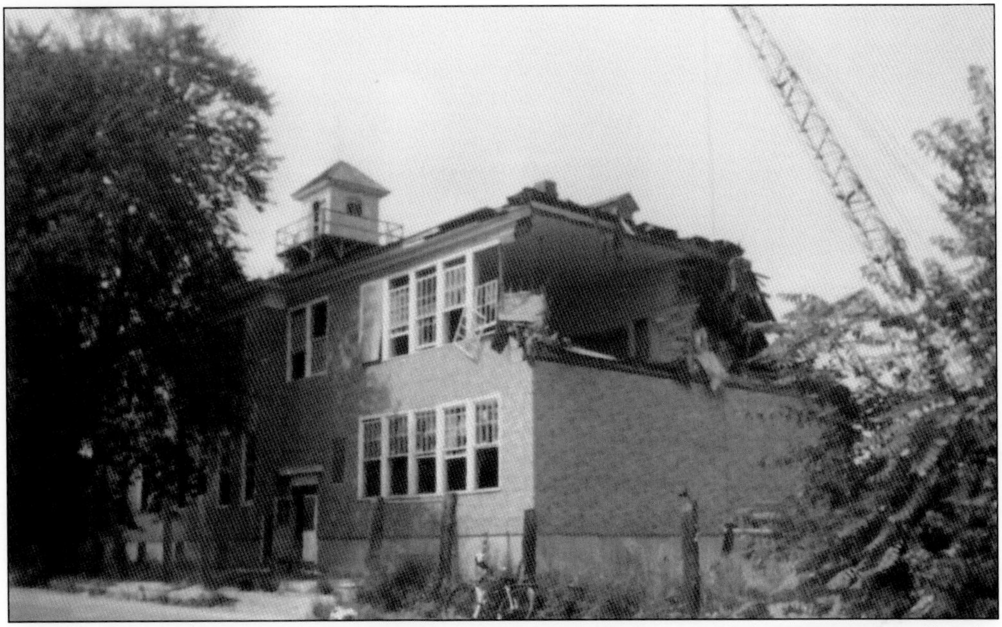

The wrecking ball arrives. Down came the old Barnegat Primary School. It was replaced by the new school built in 1931, and was razed in 1962 because of safety issues.

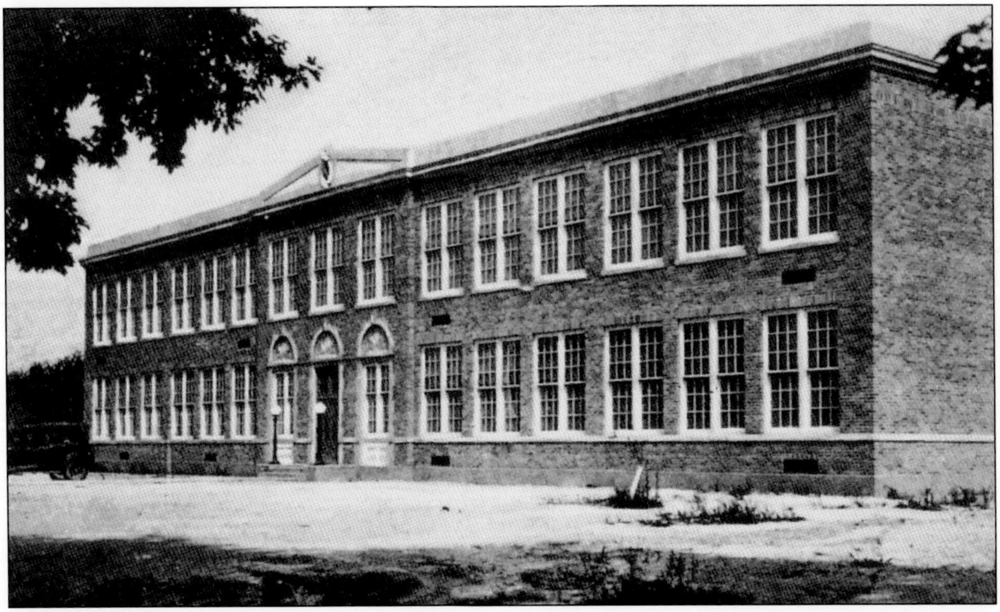

Barnegat High School. Built and dedicated in 1931, the new Barnegat High School was used until 1957. It later became the Elizabeth V. Edwards Grade School, located on North Main Street.

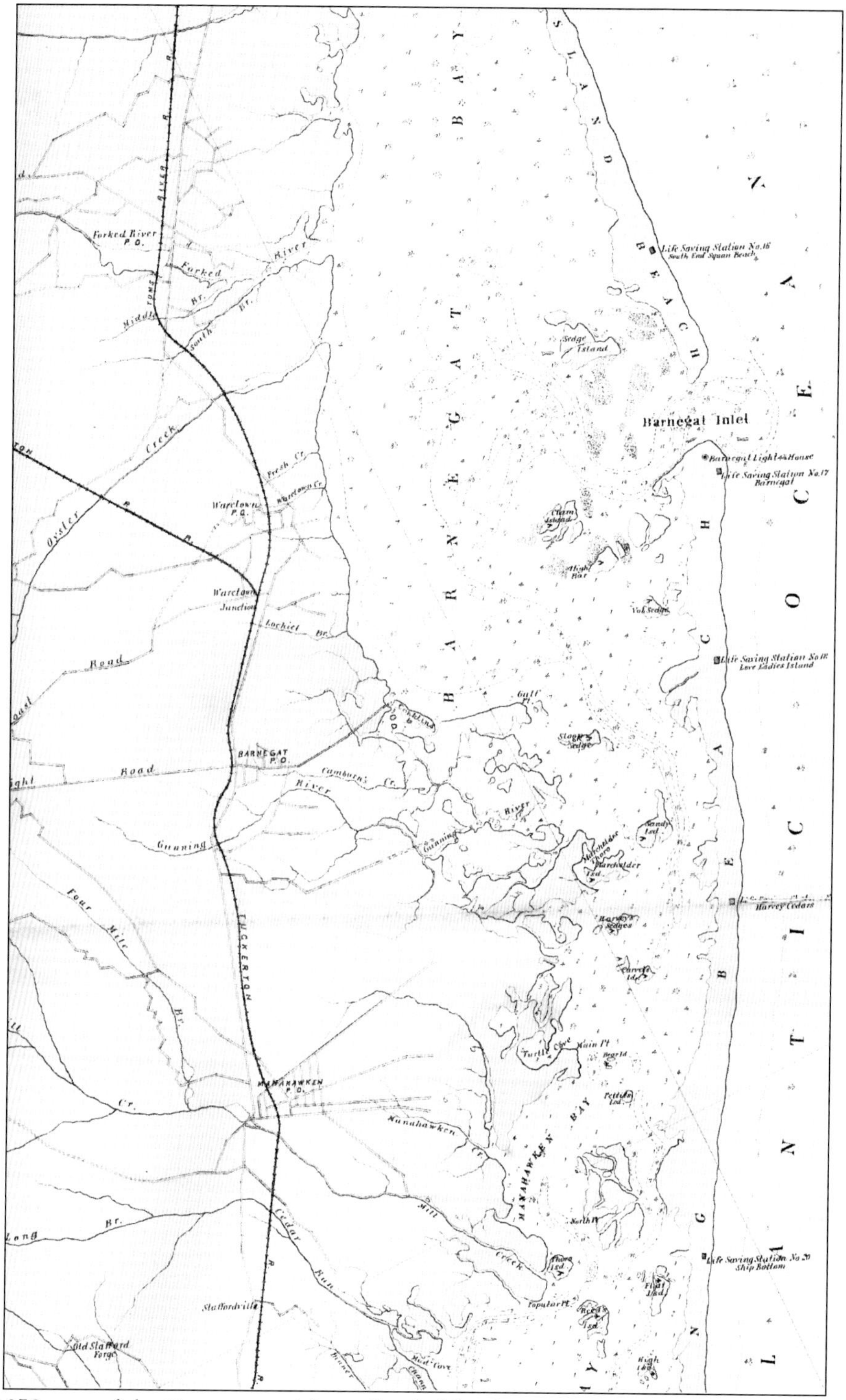

A c. 1878 map of the Barnegat and Long Beach Island area. Note the "Life Saving Stations" labeled on the oceanfront to Barnegat's east and the Tuckerton Railroad that connected Barnegat to points north and south.

Five

On the Bay

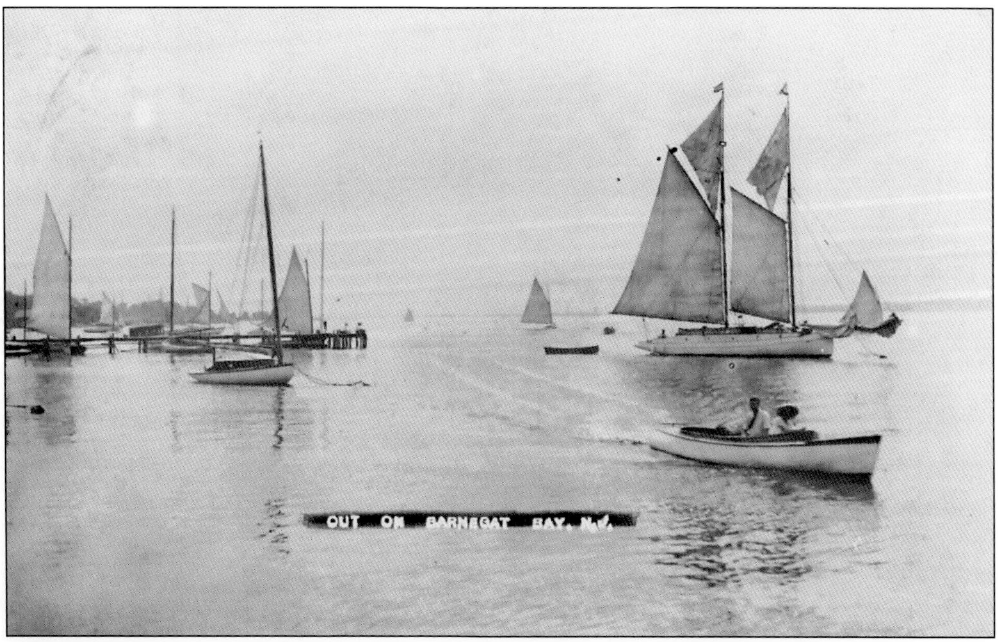

A 1911 postcard view of ships sailing on the bay. Boating was a favorite pastime of many, as it remains today.

GUIDE TO THE

"SPORTSMAN'S PARADISE"

BARNEGAT

ON THE FAMOUS BARNEGAT BAY

NEW JERSEY

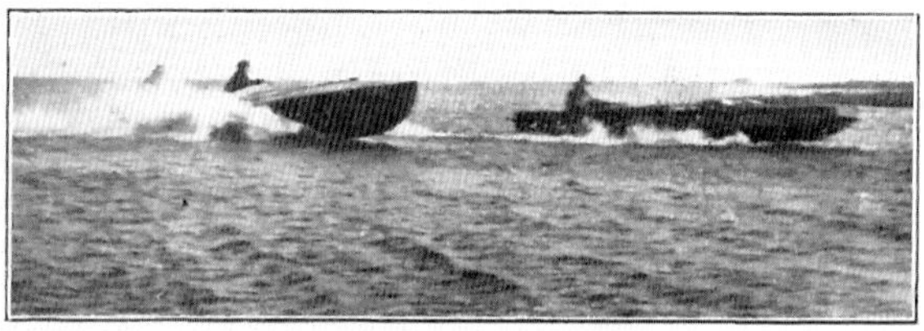

AN IDEAL PLACE TO SPEND YOUR VACATION
WHETHER IT BE SUMMER OR WINTER

PUBLISHED BY

EXCHANGE CLUB OF BARNEGAT

MEETS EVERY MONDAY AT 6 P. M. AFFILIATED WITH NATIONAL EXCHANGE

Barnegat: A "Sportsman's Paradise." Shielded by Long Beach Island on the east, Barnegat Bay was ideal for boating, fishing, crabbing, and hunting. Sportsmen came from far away to stay in local hotels and be guided by locals to favorite hunting and fishing spots.

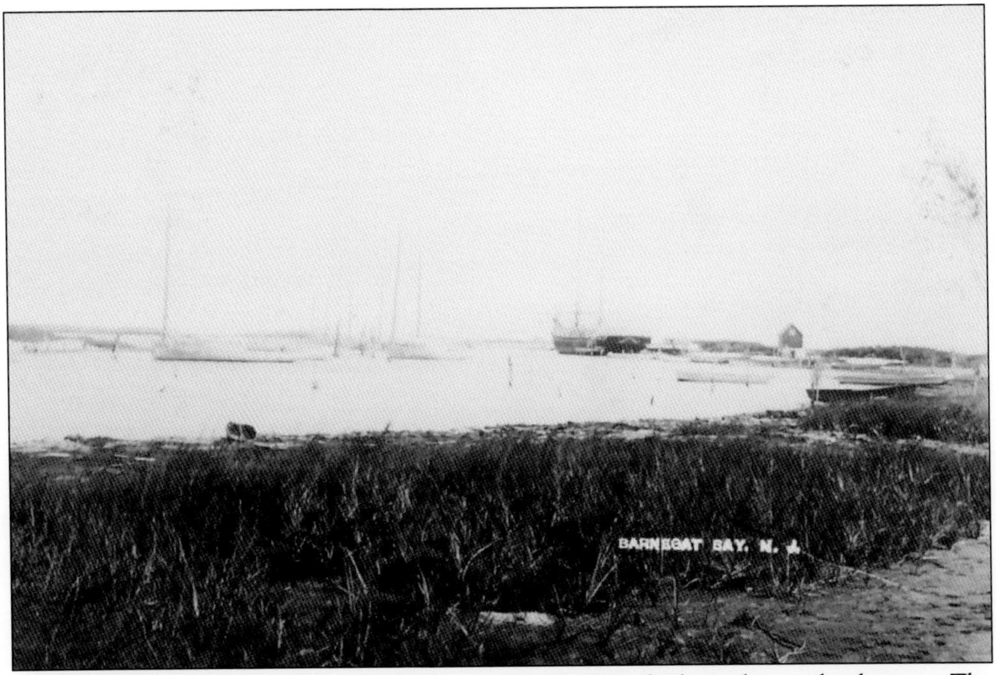

A view of the meadows on Barnegat Bay around 1910. Note the large ship in the distance. The shipping of salt hay and other local products was important to Barnegat's economy, as was the building of boats and ships.

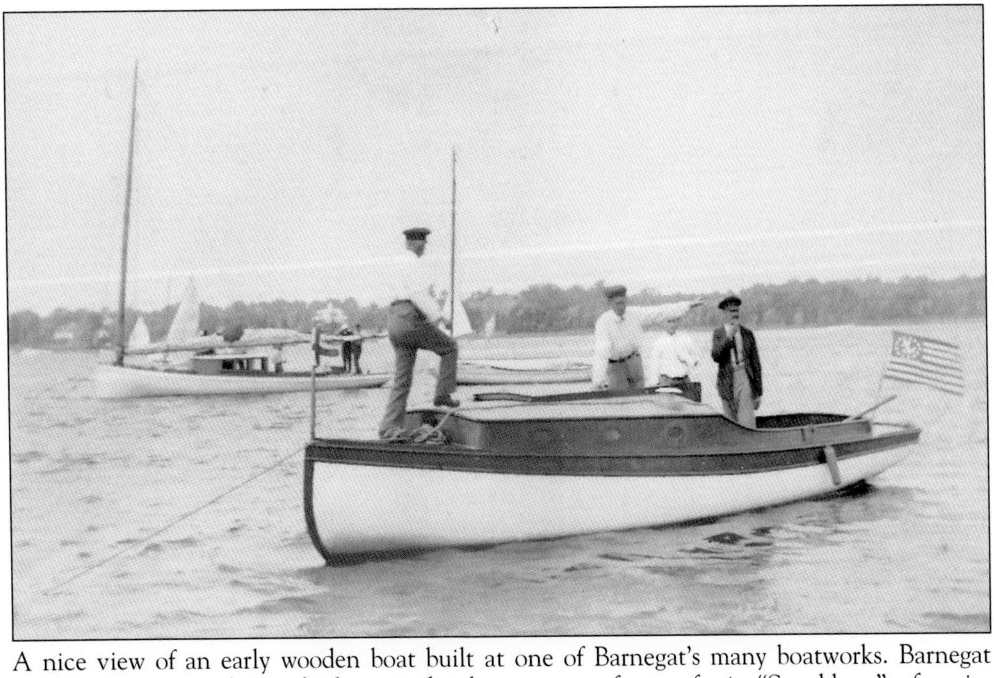

A nice view of an early wooden boat built at one of Barnegat's many boatworks. Barnegat produced many wooden craft; the township became most famous for its "Sneakbox," a favorite of local duck hunters.

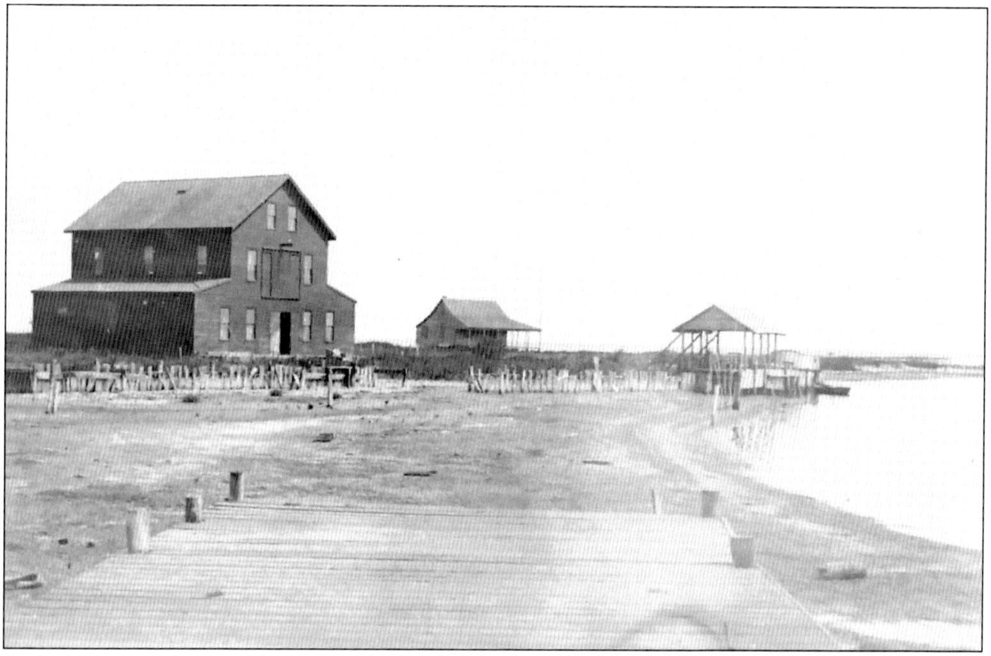

A 1910 view of the old salt hay building on the Barnegat shore. Salt hay was a valuable commodity, harvested and sold for packing valuable glassware and china.

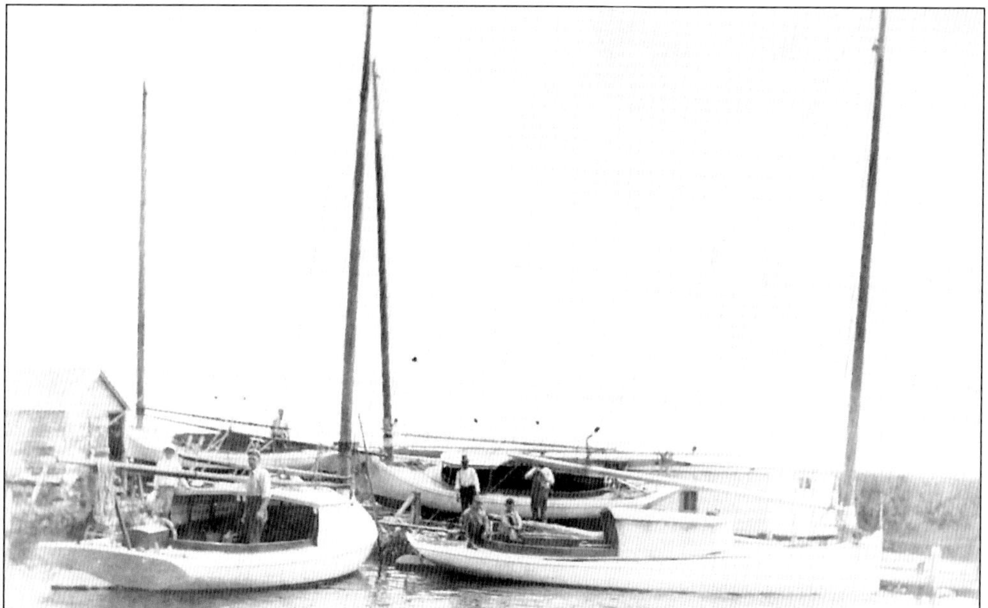

The landing at Barnegat around 1911. Several sizes of wooden crafts are shown. Many were built in Barnegat using local timbers, by local craftsman.

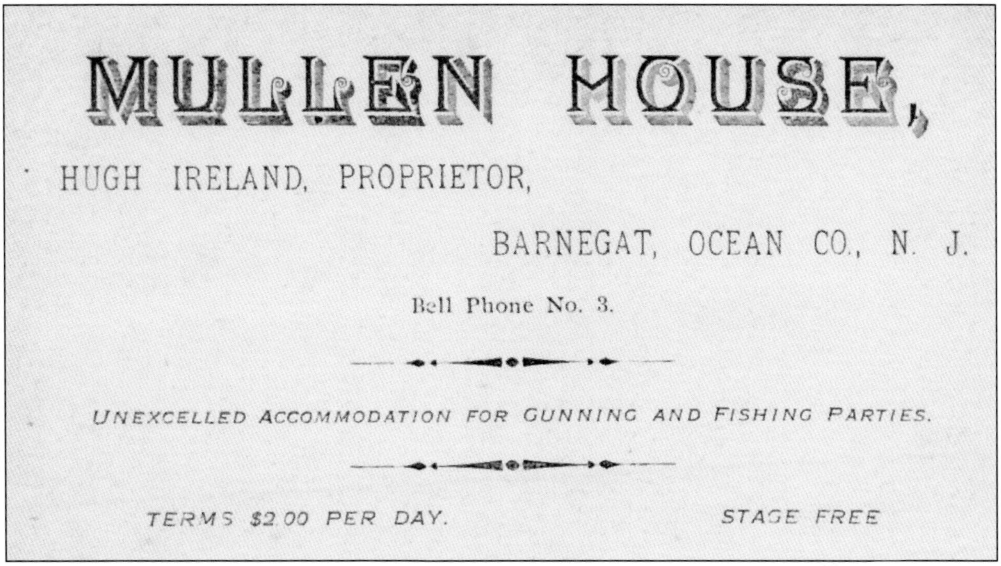

The development of tourism. The hotel industry thrived on the tourist trade, filling every available room in season. A free stage from the train to the hotel was usually provided.

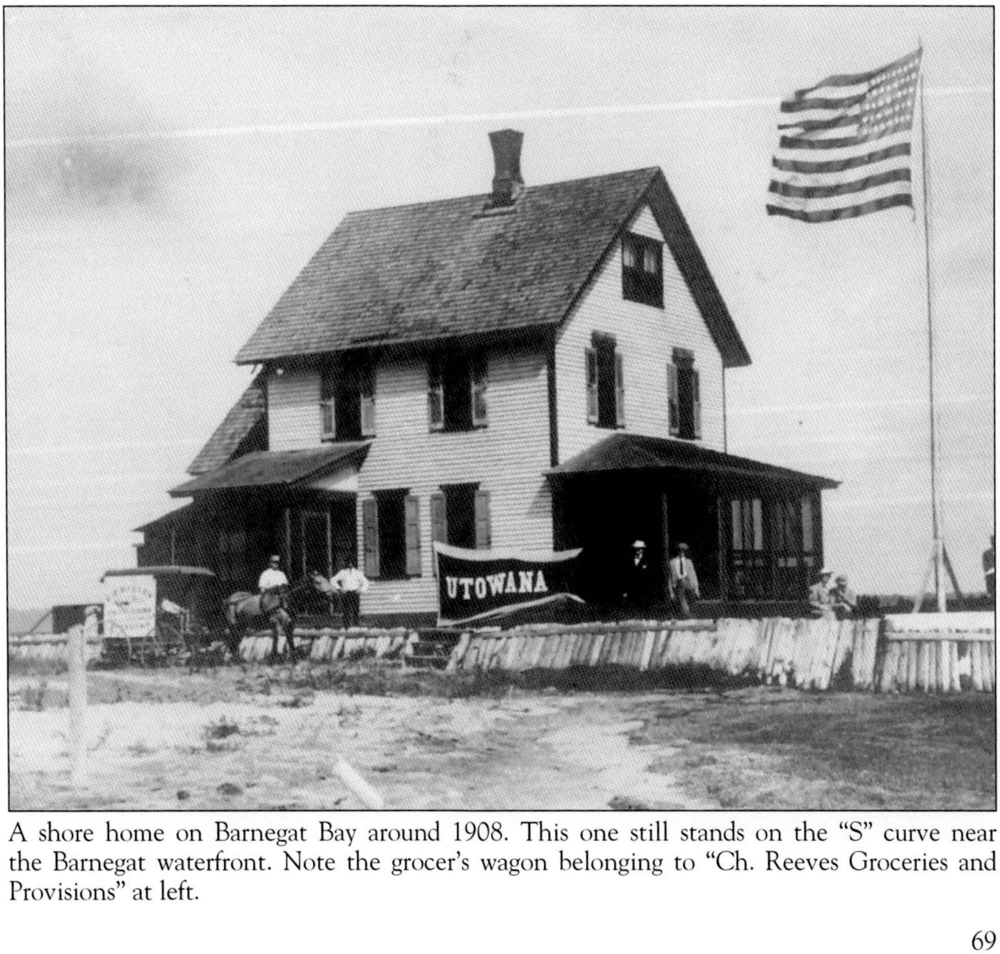

A shore home on Barnegat Bay around 1908. This one still stands on the "S" curve near the Barnegat waterfront. Note the grocer's wagon belonging to "Ch. Reeves Groceries and Provisions" at left.

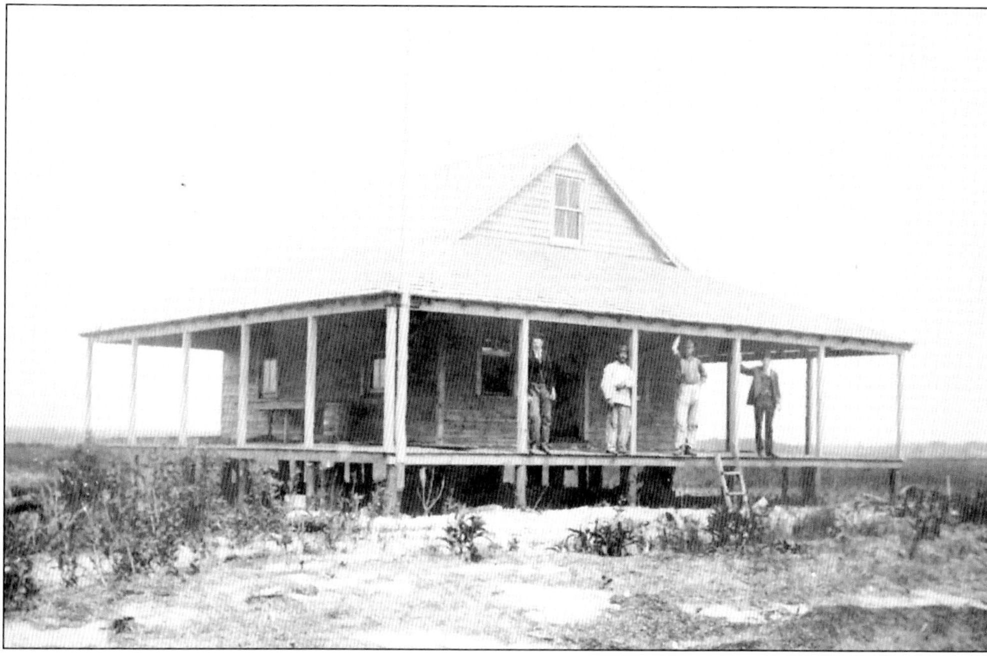

A 1908 view of the Barnegat Yacht Club, which was built in 1905. Clubs such a this one formed to promote the increasingly popular hobbies of yachting and boat racing. Shown here are a few locals: "Papa" Collins, Amos Bahr, Will Bowker, and Alex Chandler.

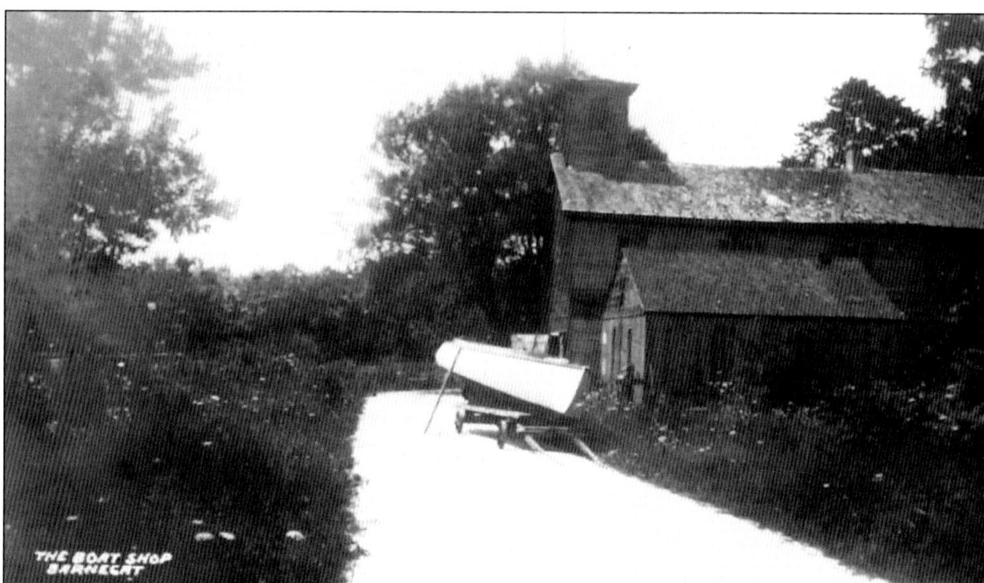

A 1919 view of the Perrine Boat Shop, originator of the famous Perrine "Sneakbox." Built originally as a school in 1867 and used as such until 1901, it is rumored to have served also as a church. J.H. Perrine purchased the building in 1901, and he produced an estimated four thousand boats here from that year until 1956. The building was torn down in 1970.

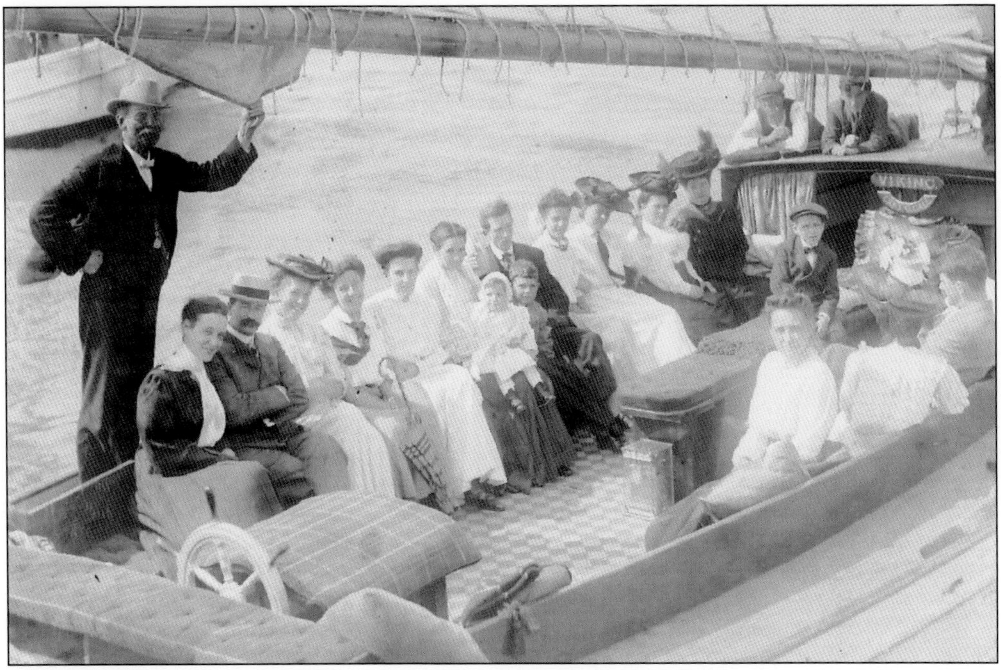

The ship *Viking* on Barnegat Bay *c.* 1914. Piloted by Captain G. Gale, it served as a pleasure and charter boat in the local waters.

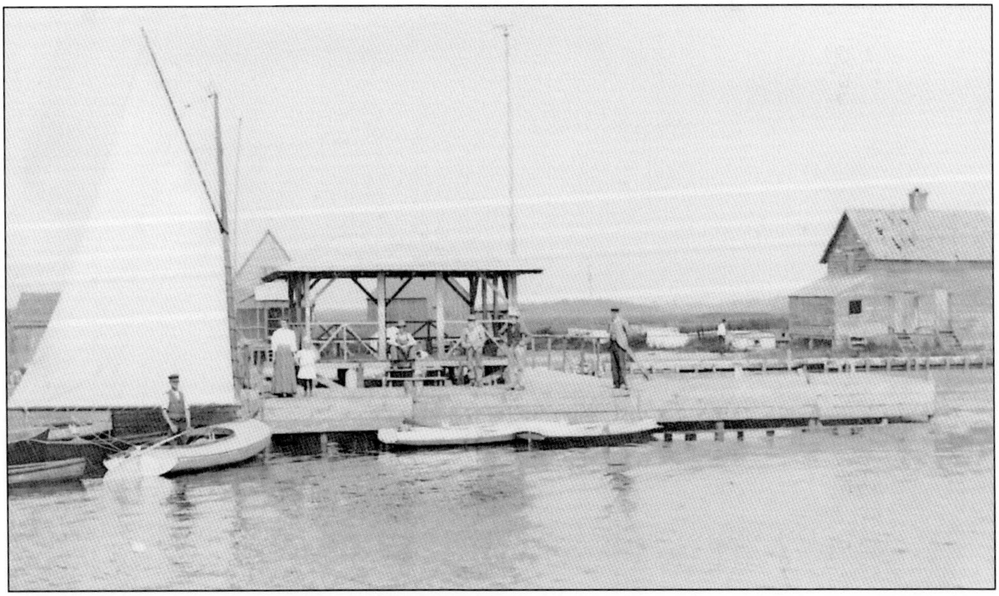

A *c.* 1910 view of the pavilion on the Barnegat waterfront. Many pavilions were built here through the years to shade visitors from the hot summer sun. A longtime gathering spot for local residents, it was known as a cool place to catch up on the day's gossip.

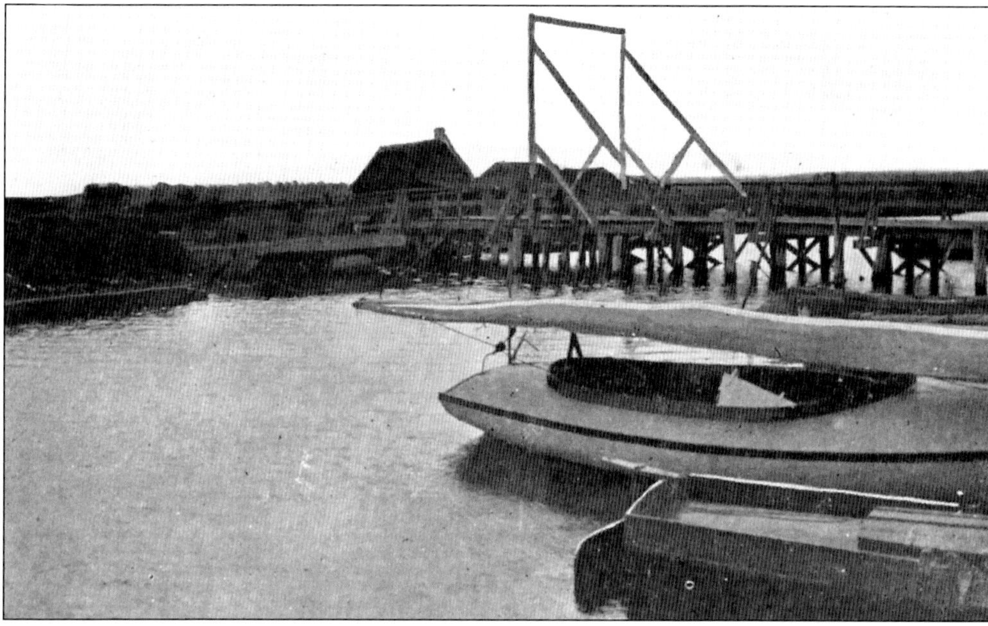

An early wooden drawbridge over Double Creek, heading toward Barnegat's dock. The oyster houses are shown in the center. This photograph was taken *c.* 1912.

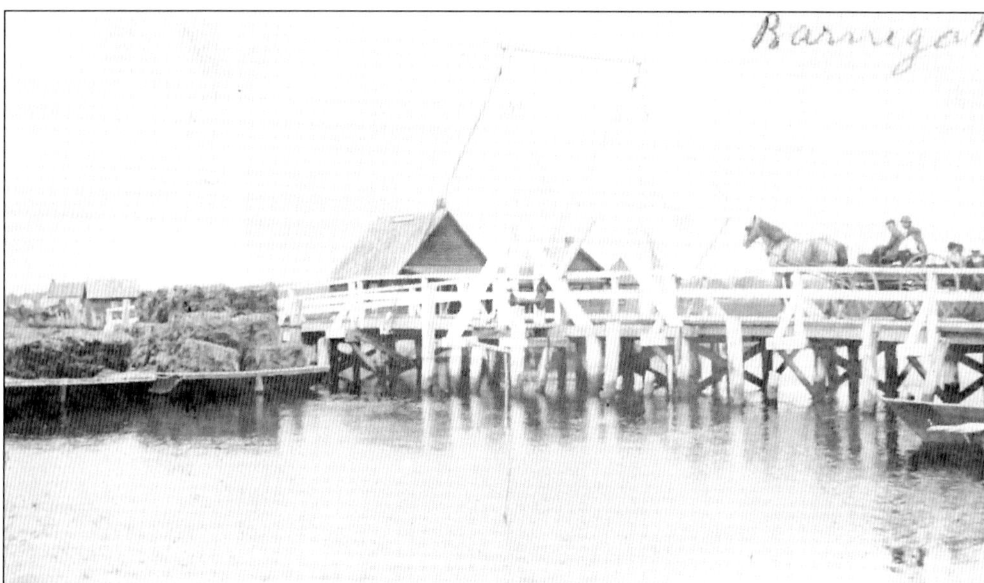

A 1909 view of the drawbridge with a horse and wagon headed toward the docks. This was a hand-operated drawbridge which used pulleys to accommodate boat traffic.

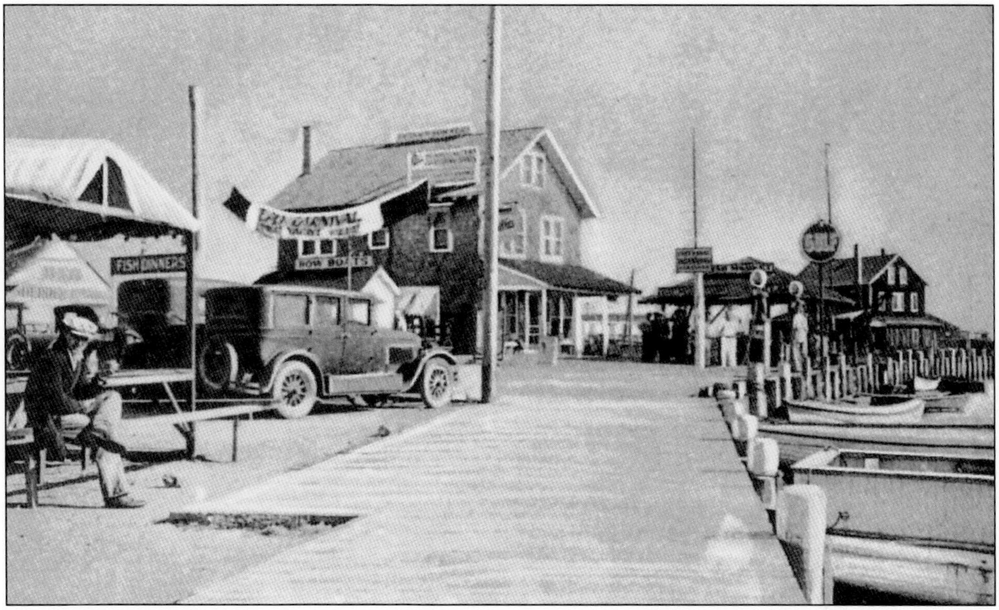

The Lower Dock at Barnegat *c.* 1932. This location was known by many local children for its excellent crabbing. The buildings at left housed several seafood restaurants.

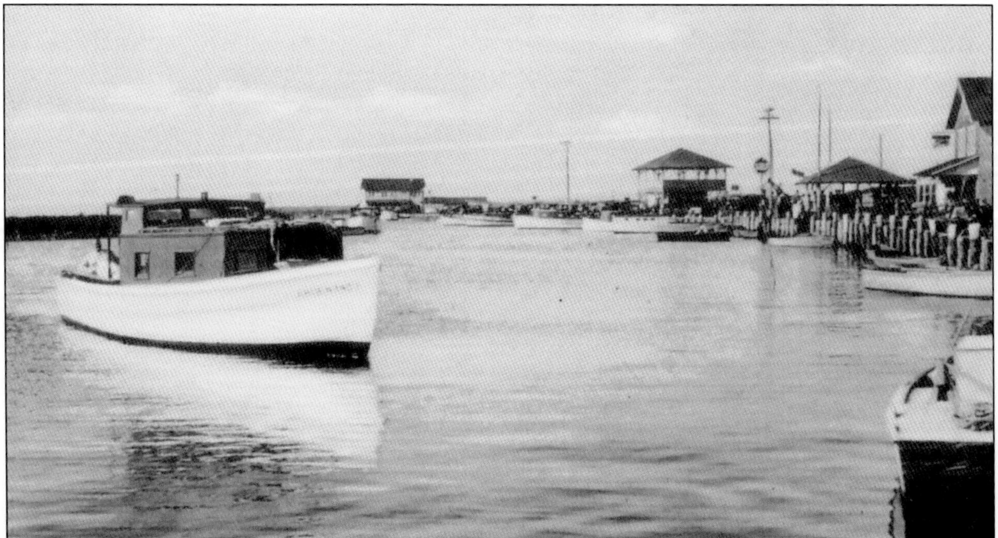

Charter boat landing at a Barnegat dock around 1930. Boats such as these served as both shuttles to Long Beach Island and for fishing excursions.

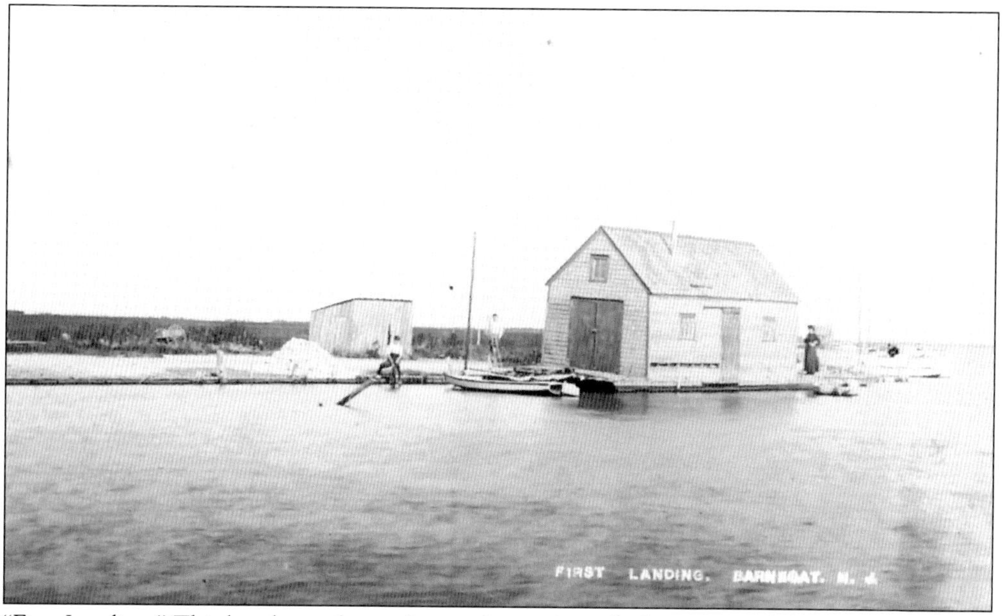

"First Landing." This boathouse housed many boats through the years and sheltered them from the elements. The photograph was taken around 1908.

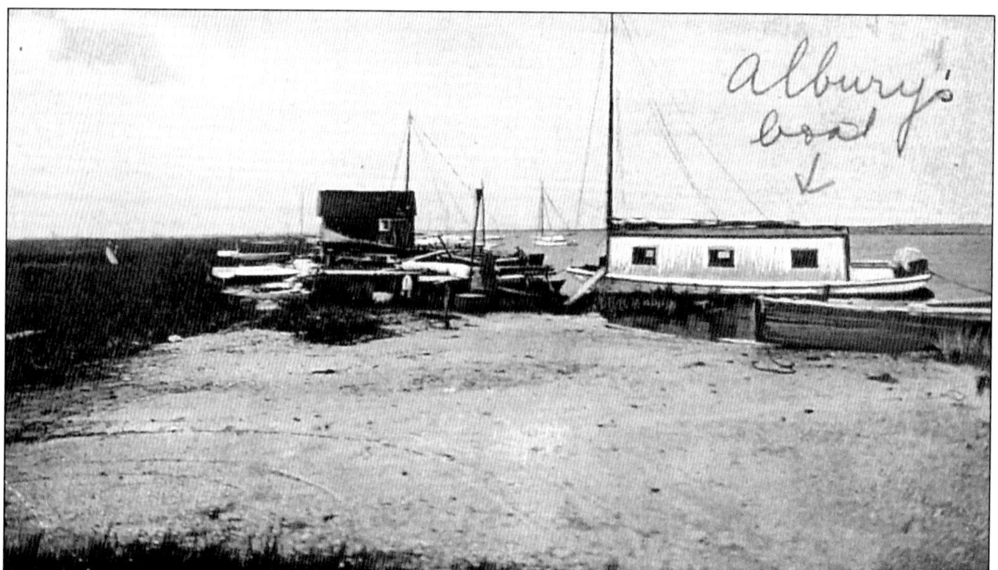

North Shore Landing and Dock. Boats such as the one shown here could sleep as many as a dozen or so guests on overnight excursions.

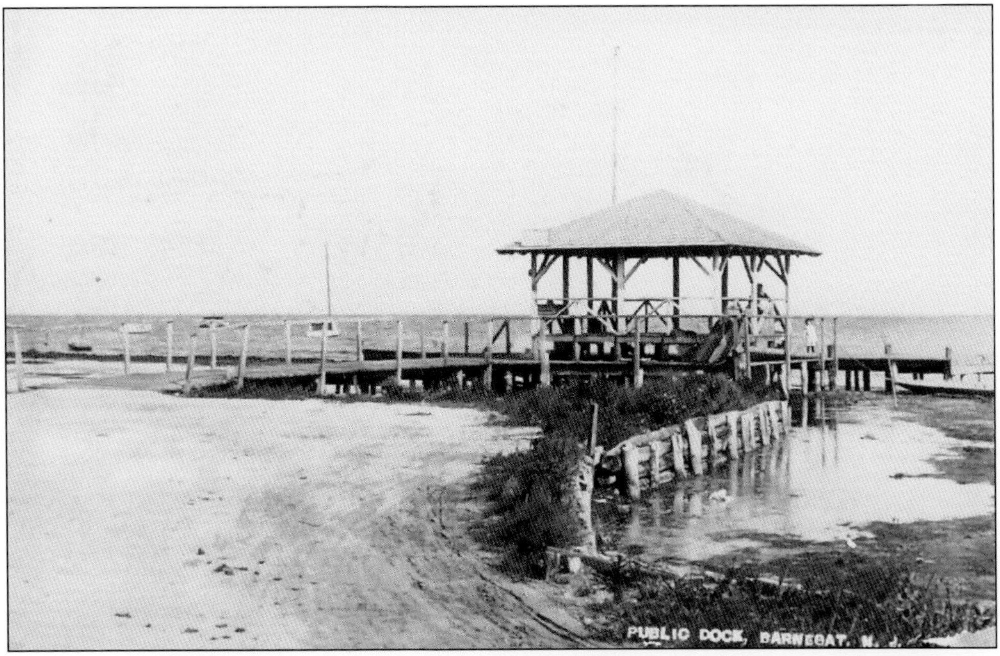

A c. 1910 view of the public dock area. On a clear day, Barnegat Lighthouse can be seen across the bay to the east.

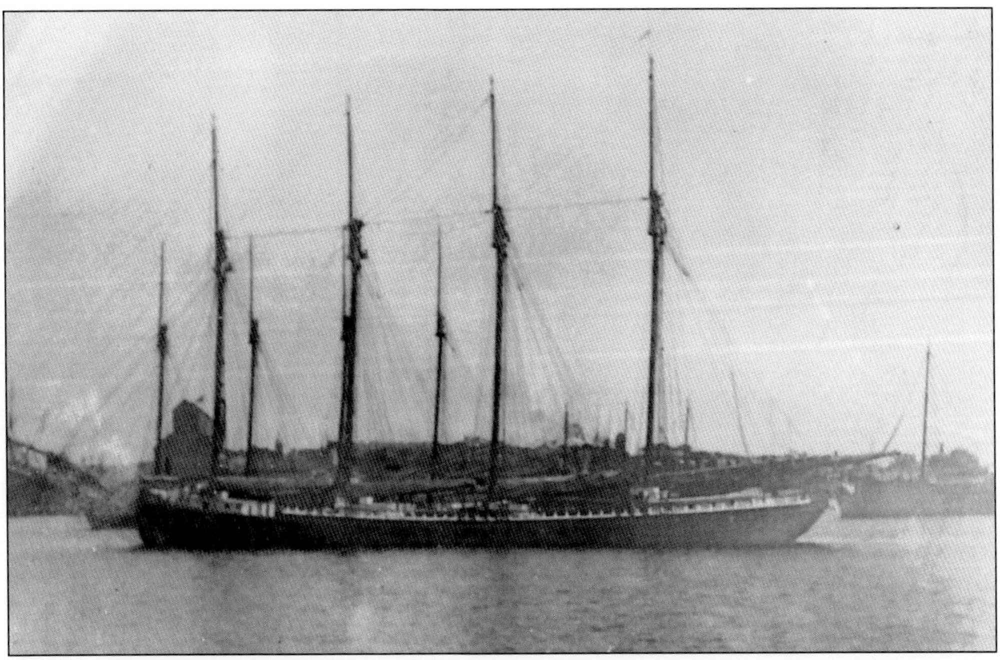

A very early view of a local ship, the schooner *Percy Birdsall* of Barnegat/Waretown, in Boston Harbor around 1899. These ships carried cargo to ports around the world, employing many local men.

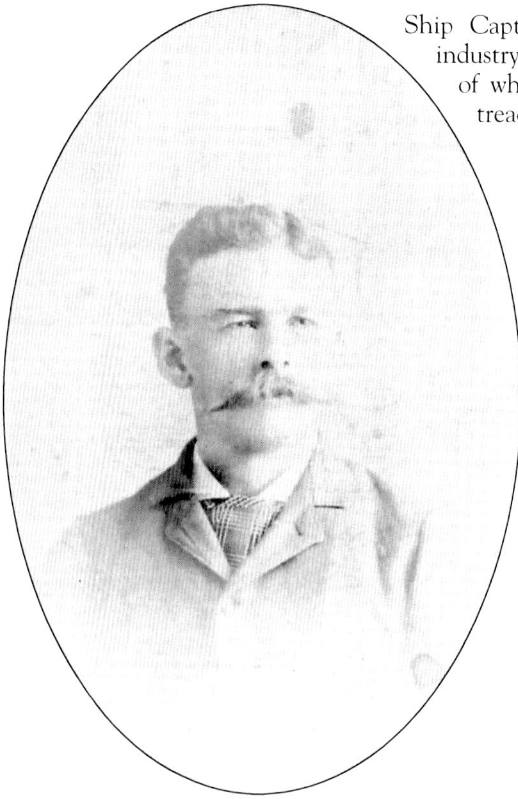

Ship Captain Henry Smith *c.* 1895. The shipping industry employed hundreds of local men, many of whom were lost at sea or shipwrecked on the treacherous Atlantic coast.

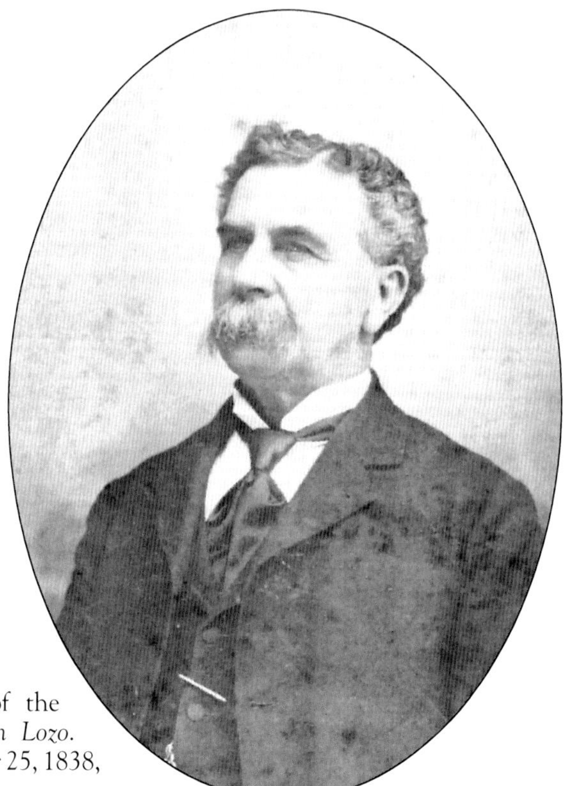

Captain William T. Fitz Randolph of the schooners *T. Morris Perot* and *Stephen Lozo*. Captain Randolph was born on December 25, 1838, and died in 1910.

Captain Bennington F. Randolph. This Captain Randolph piloted the schooner *Francis Halleck* out of Barnegat Bay. He was later lost at sea.

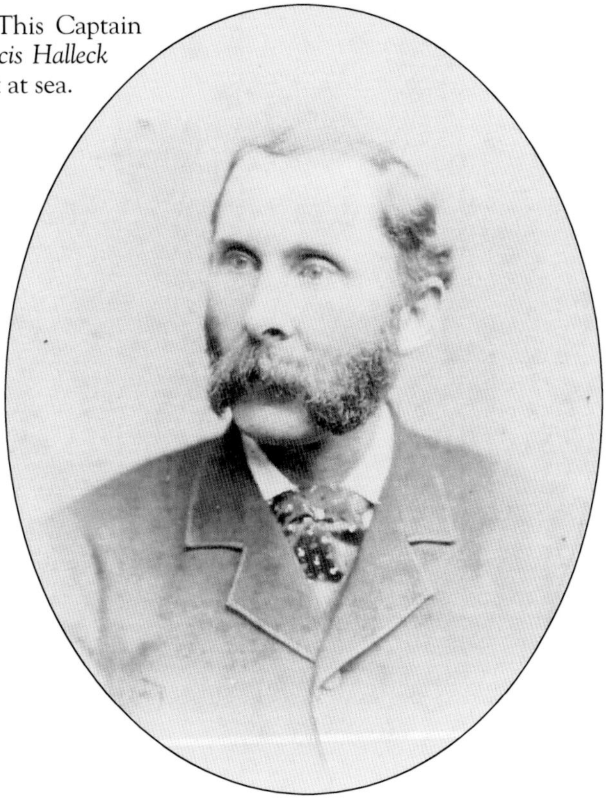

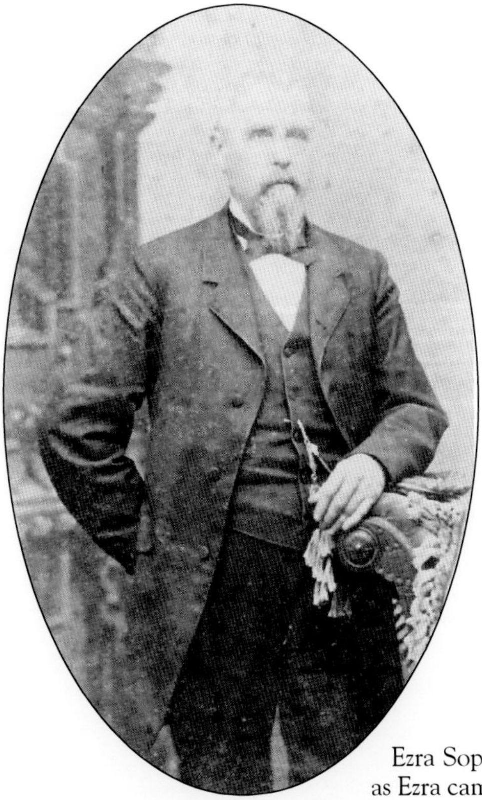

Ezra Soper, a local resident and captain. Many men such as Ezra came from a long line of seamen.

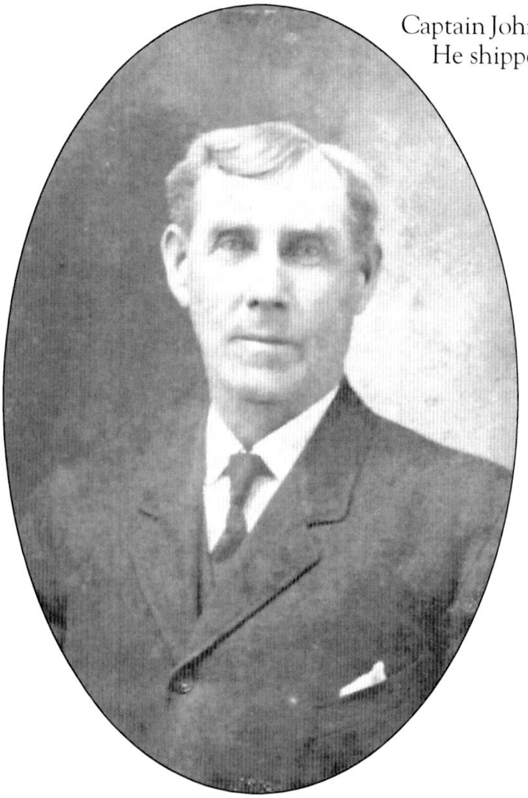

Captain John S. Hankins, another local Barnegat seaman. He shipped cargo aboard his ship, the *Jennie Richter*.

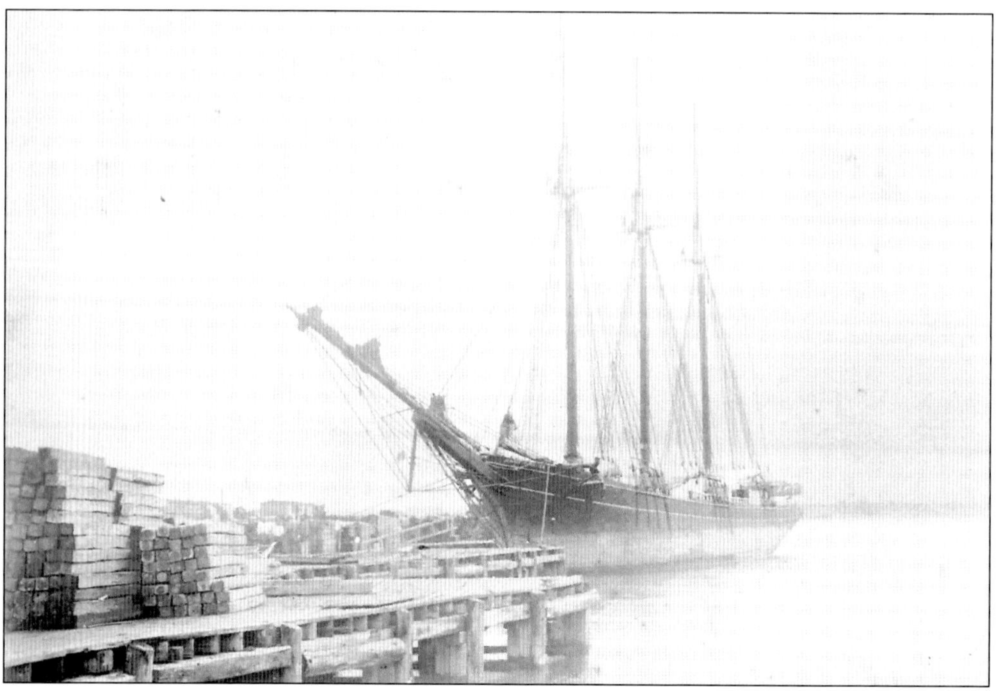

The *Jennie Richter*. Shown here unloading lumber at Jacksonville, Florida, this schooner was piloted by Barnegat Captain John S. Hankins. This photograph was taken on October 8, 1915.

Six

Our Neighbors

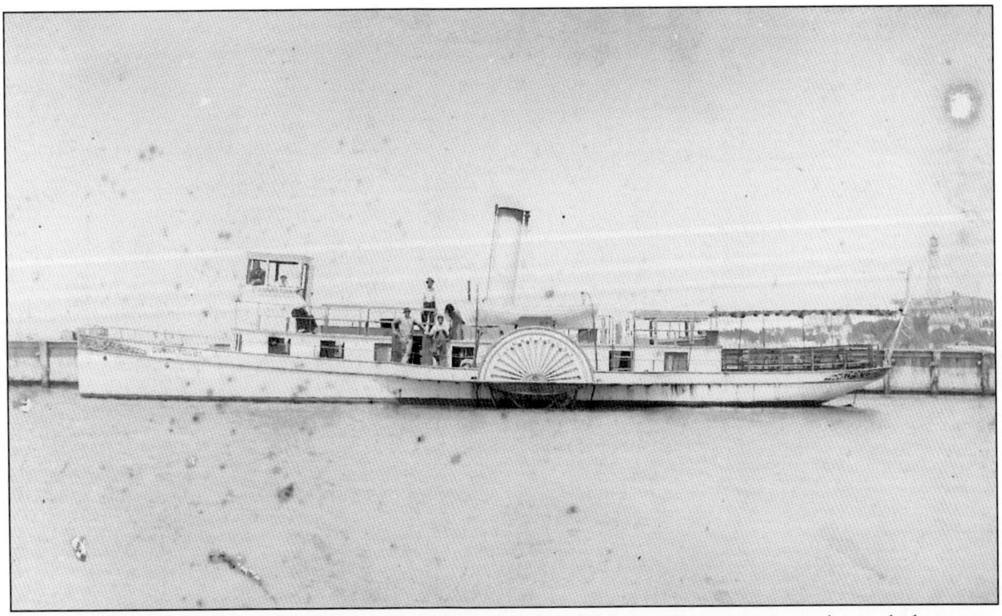

The *Connetiquot*. Barnegat even had a paddlewheel steamboat that transported people between Long Beach Island and the mainland. The *Connetiquot* traveled between Barnegat, Barnegat City (Barnegat Light), and Barnegat Pier to pick up train passengers before 1885. Note the Barnegat Lighthouse in the right background.

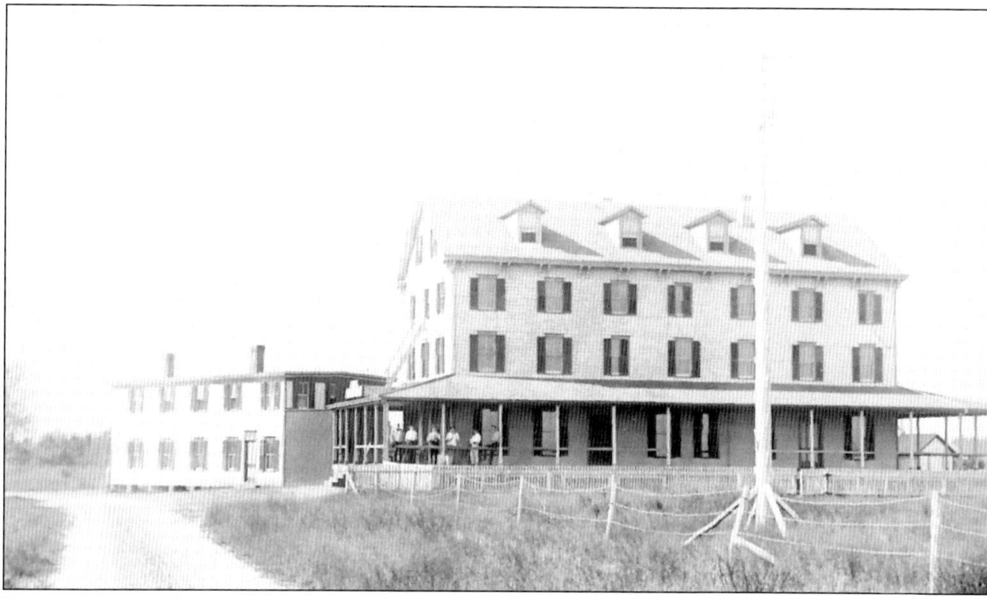

Barnegat's neighbor to the north. Waretown was also known for its several large hotels and bay life. Shown here is the Bayview Hotel *c.* 1908.

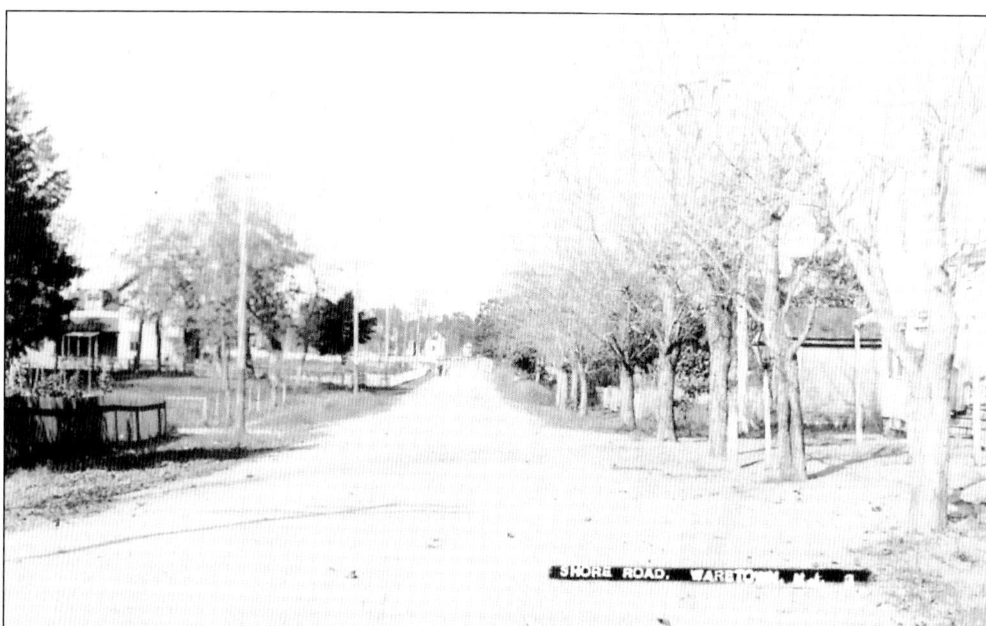

Shore Road (Main Street) in the center of Waretown proper. This *c.* 1913 photograph looks north at Bay Road and was taken by the Howell photographer named Merriman.

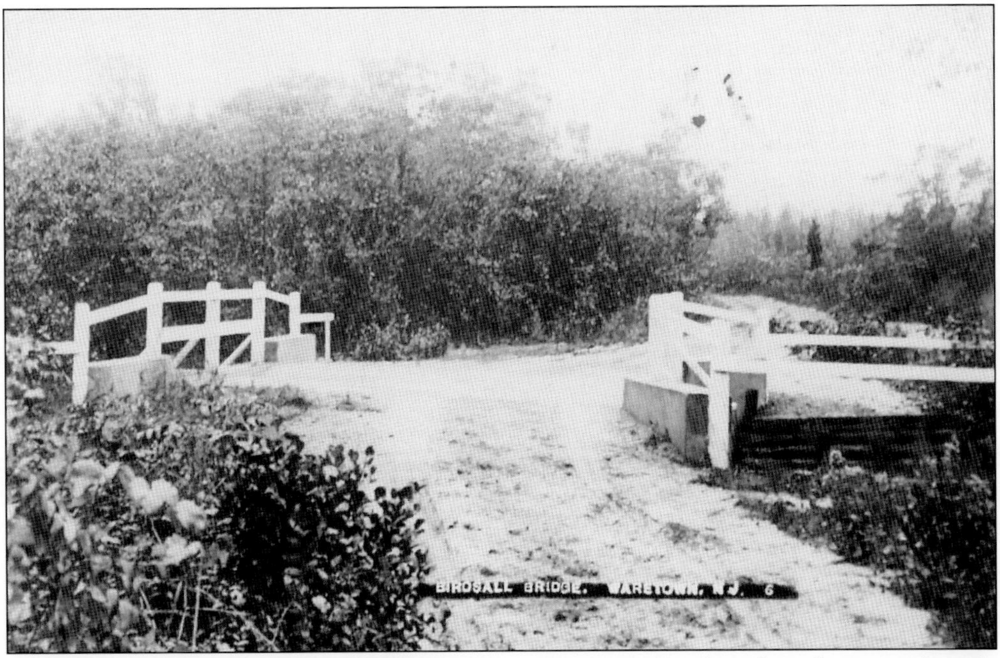

A 1908 view of the old wooden Birdsall Bridge in Waretown. Roads such as these were heavily traveled by horse and wagon, and rain-drenched roads often made for hazardous travel.

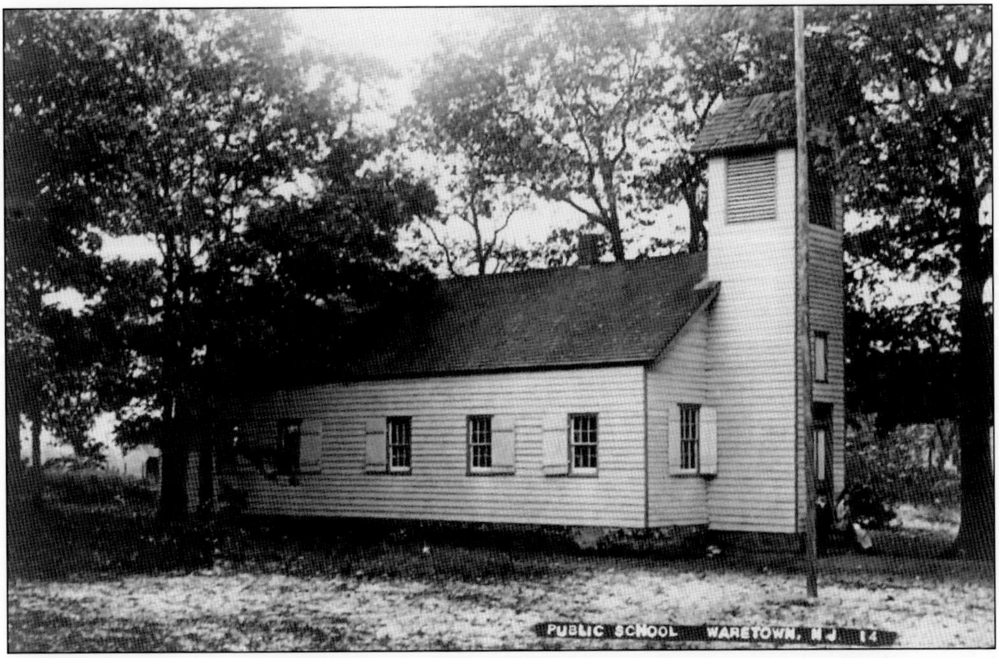

A 1910 postcard of the public school at Waretown. Originally a one-room schoolhouse and later converted to two classrooms, it continued in operation until 1957. The building was razed in 1969.

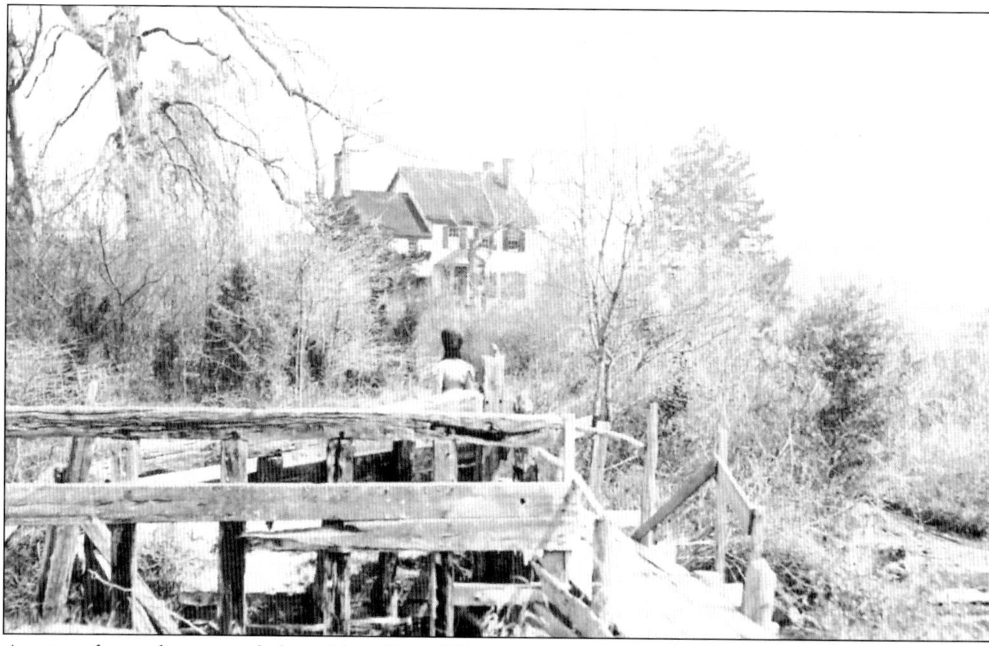

A view from the site of the old mill at Waretown. Seen in the background is the Birdsall Homestead around 1905. This was the site of a dam or sluice that provided the power for the mill; it is rumored to have originally been built by Abraham Waeir.

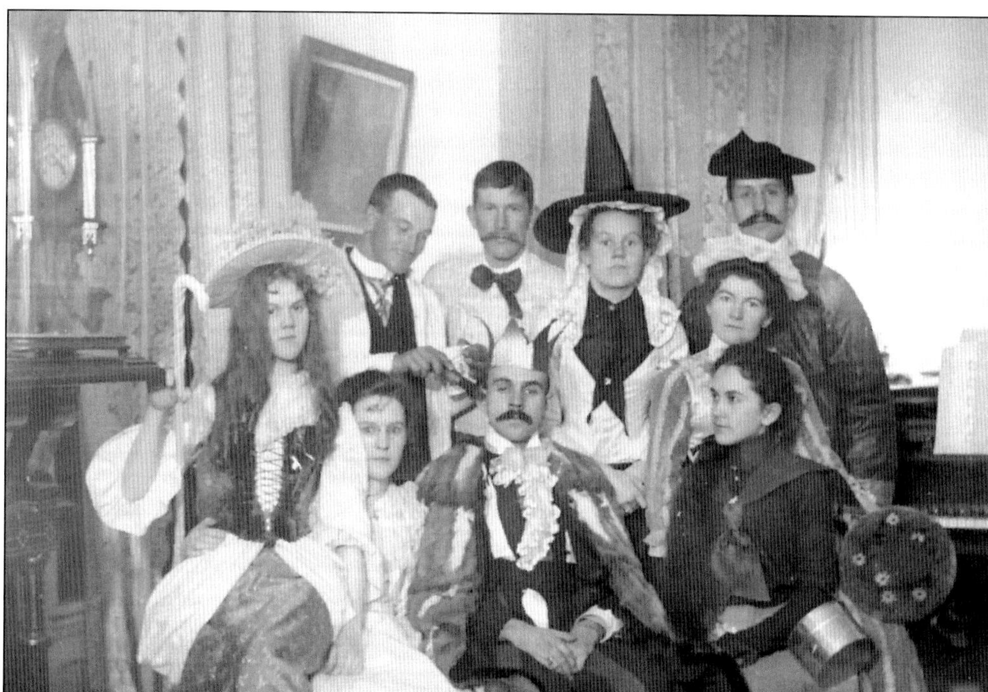

A 1910 interior view of a "Mother Goose Party" at Waretown. These parties were similar to costume and Halloween parties, but were held throughout the year.

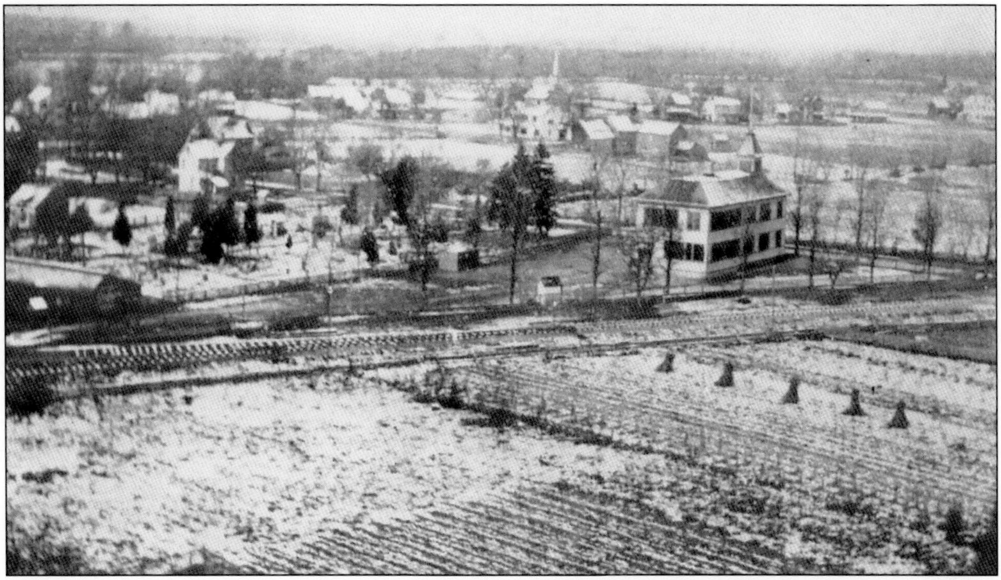

Barnegat and Waretown's neighbor to the south: Manahawkin. This 1915 bird's-eye view shows the town's center.

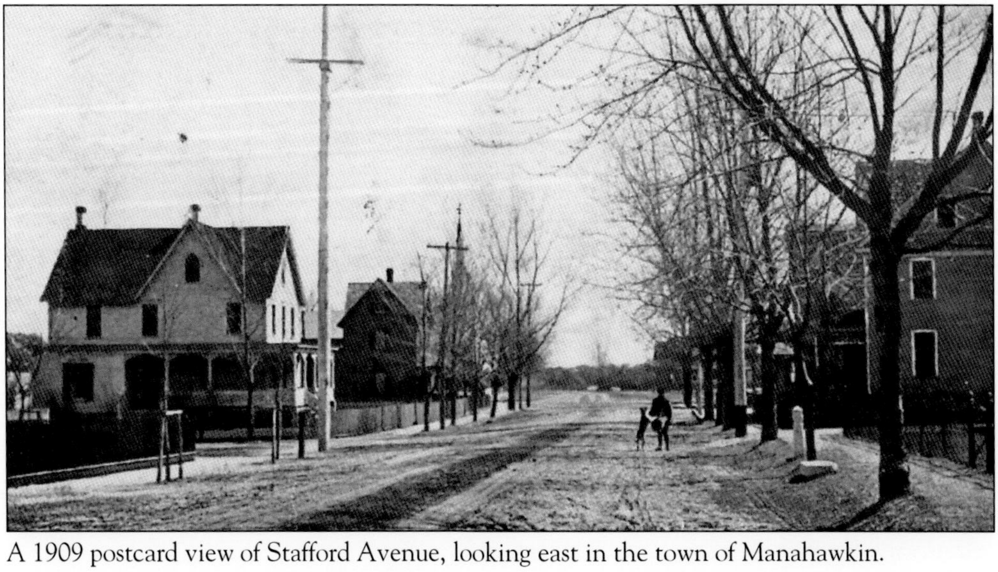

A 1909 postcard view of Stafford Avenue, looking east in the town of Manahawkin.

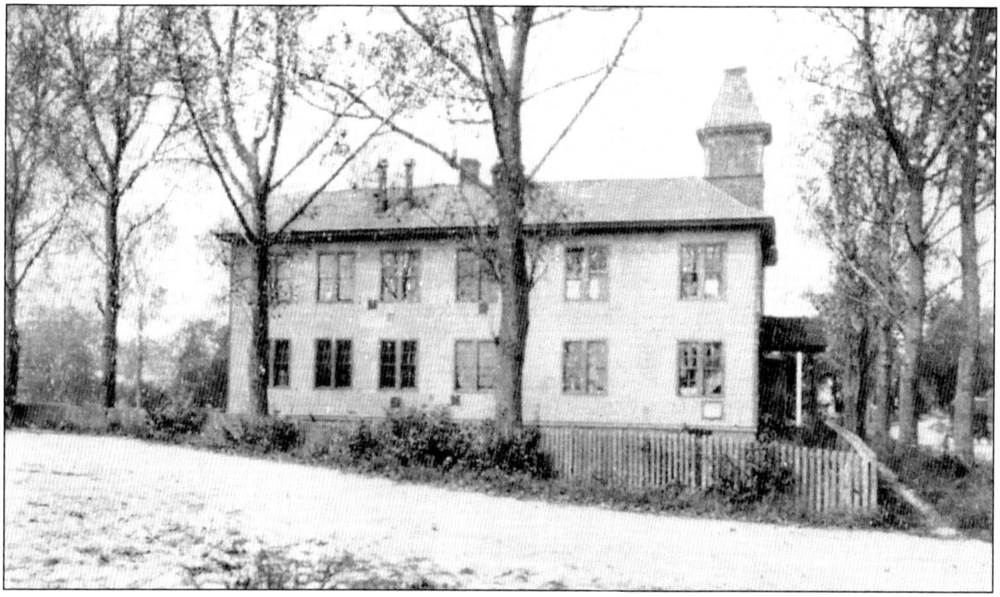

A historic schoolhouse. Originally, a one-room school stood on this site in the 1840s. This new public school at Manahawkin was built on the same site in 1887 as a two-room school. Later, a third room and eventually a fourth room were added. When the school closed in 1951, it contained five rooms.

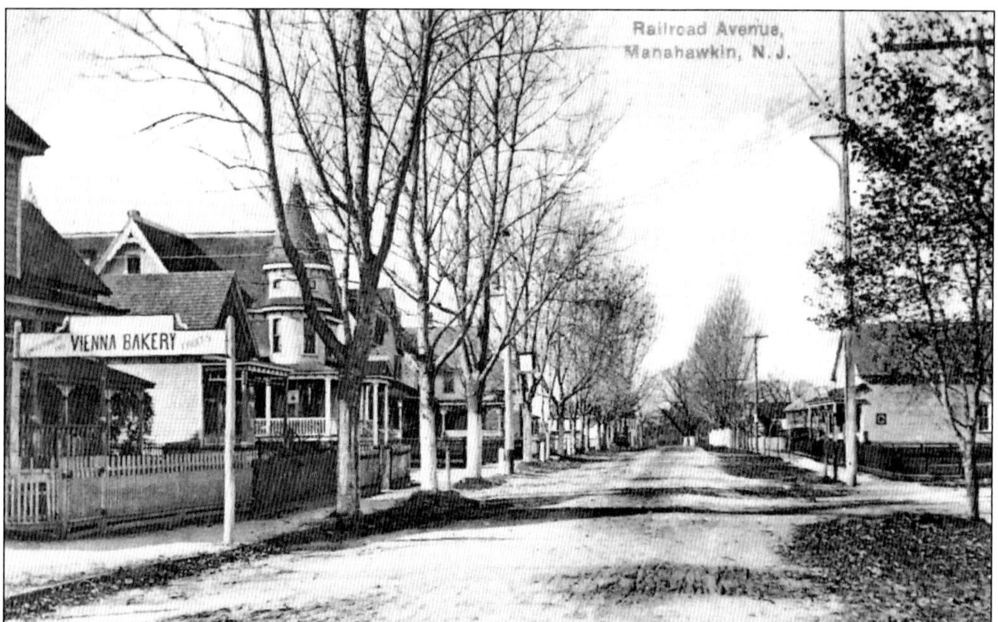

Another early view of Manahawkin around 1908, showing Railroad Avenue. Note the Vienna Bakery at the left. Manahawkin had a fairly large business district, where all the amenities needed for a comfortable living could be purchased.

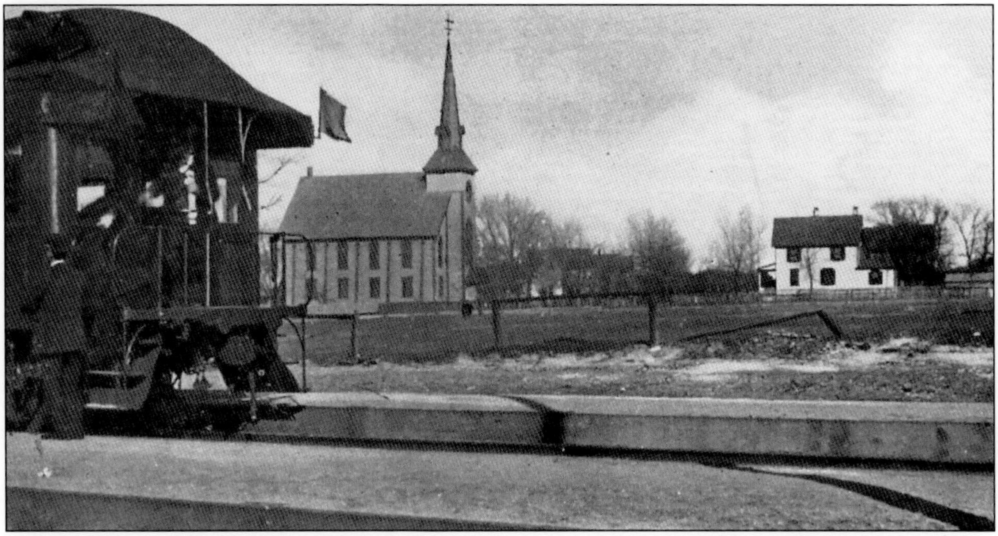

Taking off from Manahawkin. Manahawkin was connected to the popular Whiting Station via the Tuckerton Railroad. From Manahawkin ran a special line to Long Beach Island and Beach Haven. Shown here is the Methodist church from the railroad depot around 1907.

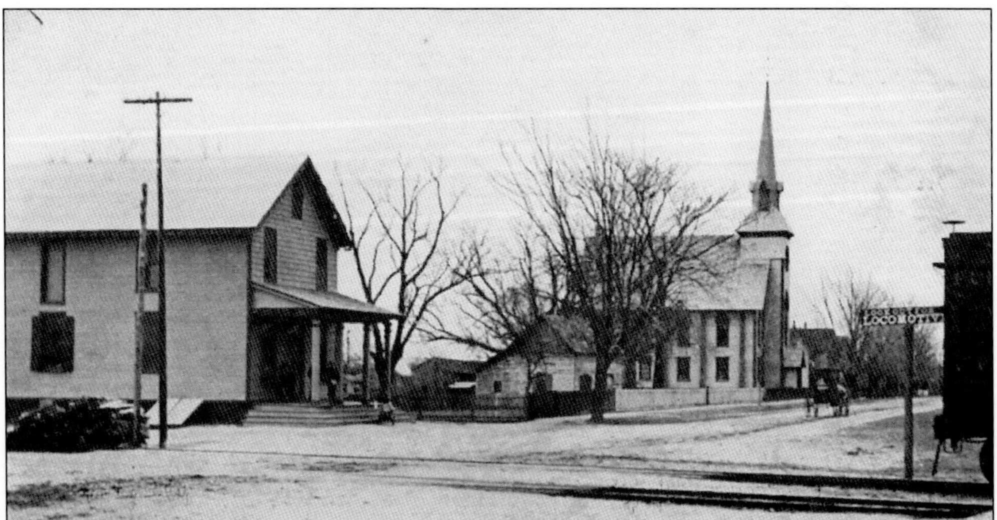

Another view of the railroad tracks at Manahawkin, passing by the Methodist church and the Manahawkin Post Office around 1907.

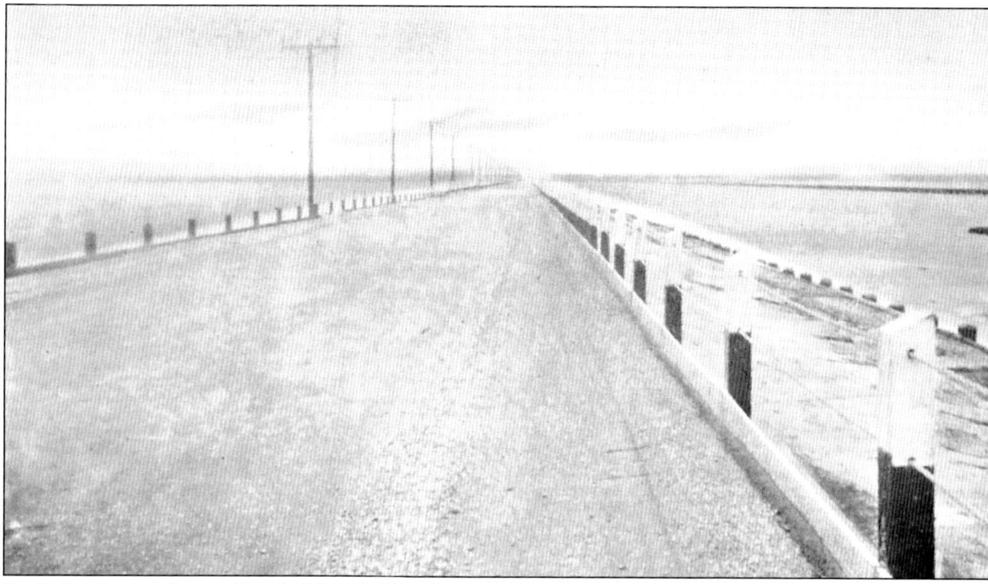

Early bridge to Long Beach Island. Heading east from Manahawkin, one quickly encounters Long Beach Island, Barnegat's neighbor across the bay. This span built in 1914 connected Manahawkin to the island.

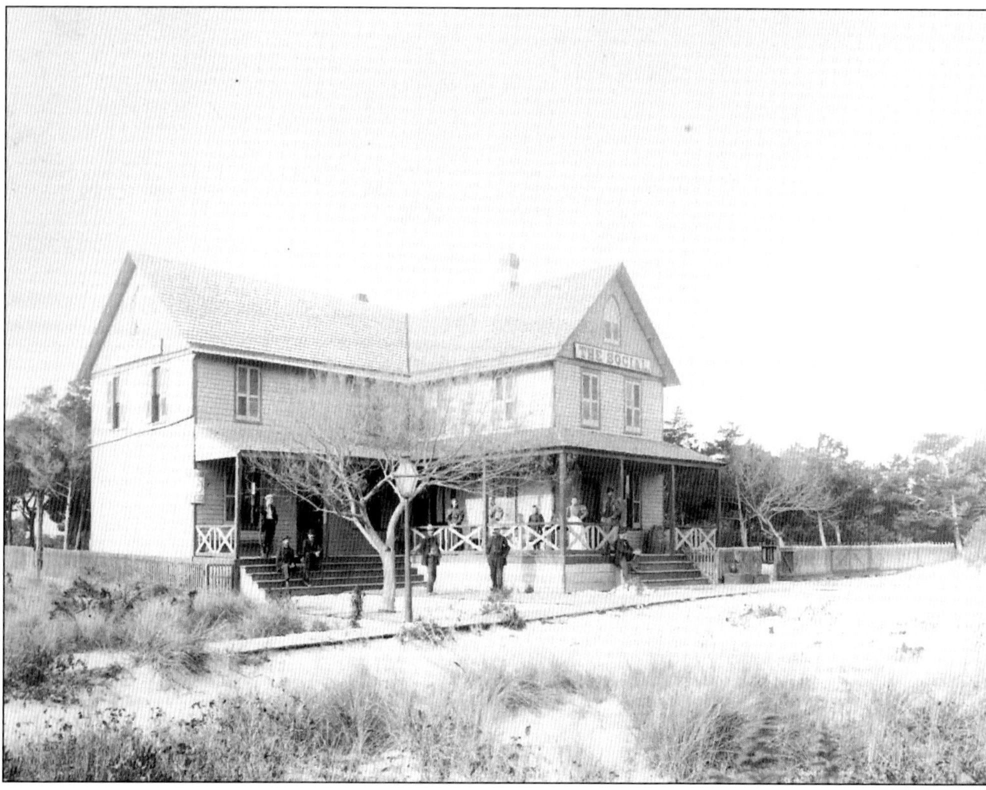

The Social. This was a boardinghouse at Barnegat City. Owned by the Kroger family for many years, it served many a sportsman during the winter months. It was during the winter months that the larger hotels normally closed for the season.

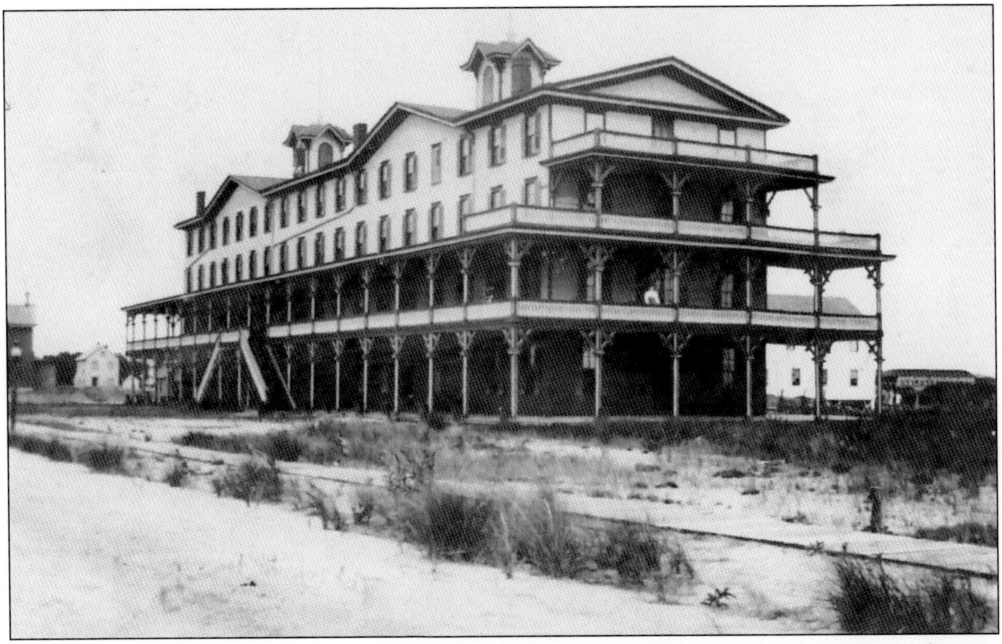

The Oceanic. The larger hotels on Long Beach Island served hundreds of visitors each year. Shown here in 1908, the Oceanic was later dismantled for lumber in 1914, when it was damaged in a storm. Today this exact area is underwater, claimed by the sea.

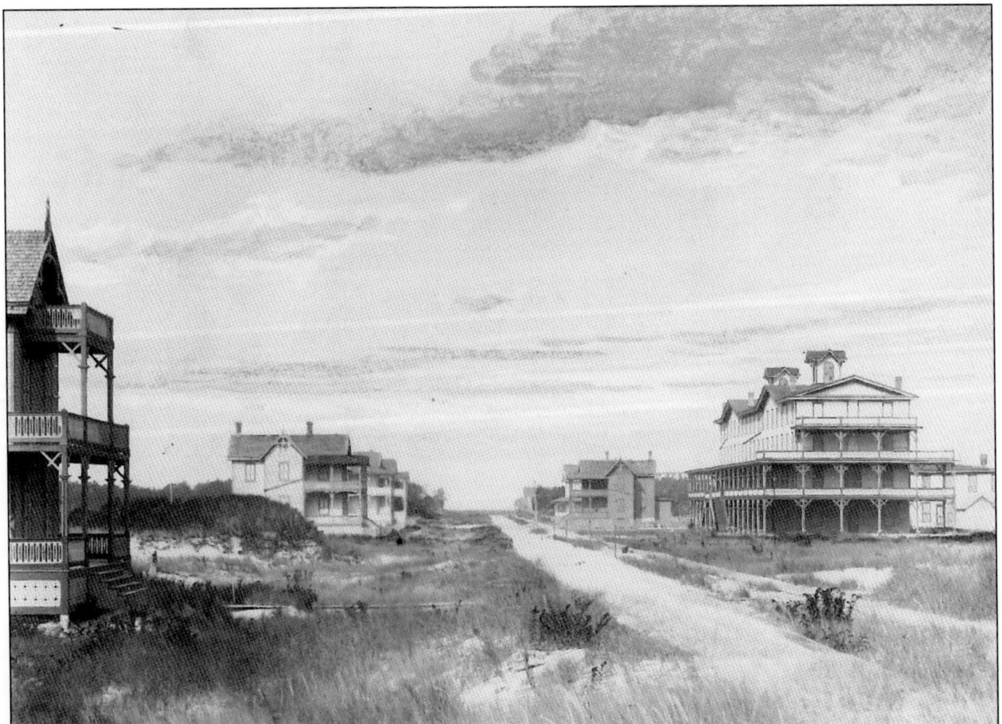

Another view of the Oceanic Hotel, this one taken around 1910. Note the primitive dirt roads and early shore architecture.

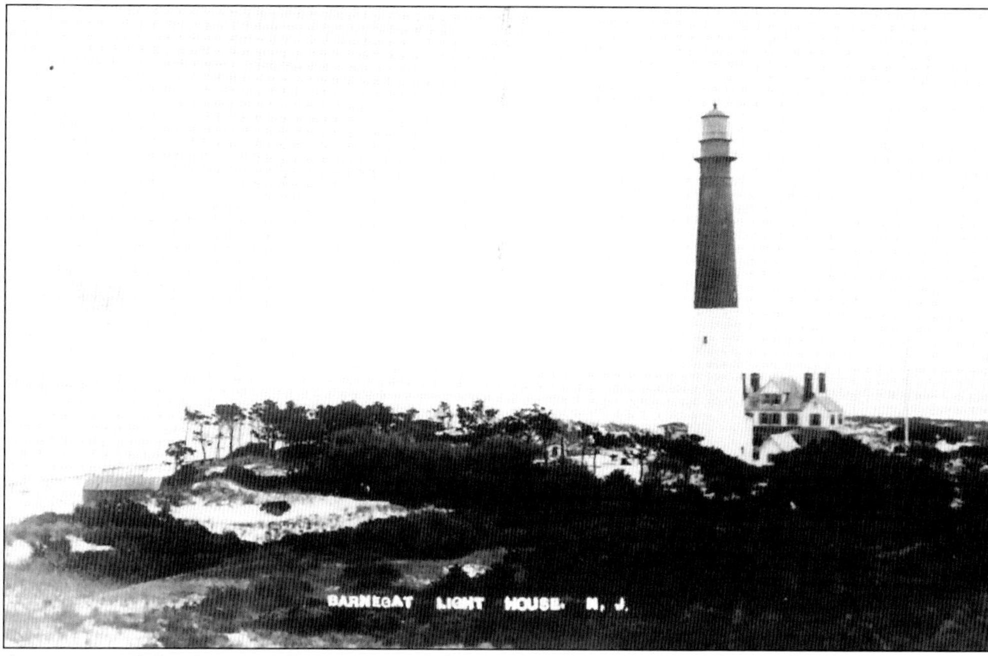

A picture of the historic Barnegat Lighthouse taken around 1913. Completed in 1858, it remained a beacon protecting ships from the treacherous shoreline until 1943. The keeper's house, shown to the right of the lighthouse, was lost to the sea in 1920.

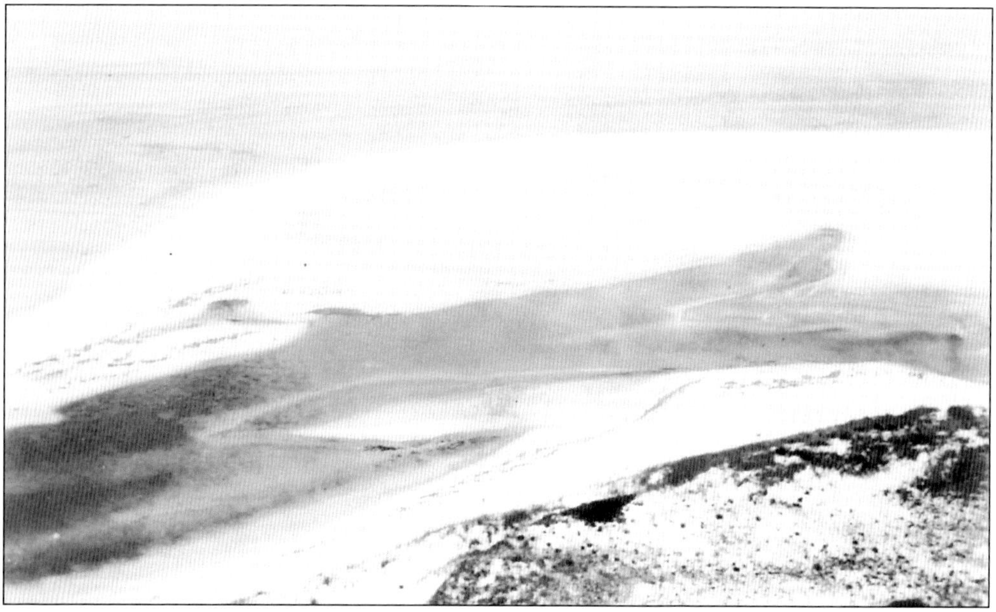

A very early view of the Barnegat Inlet taken from atop of the Barnegat Lighthouse around 1900. The height of the tower is over 160 feet above ground. The lighthouse was built at a cost of $43,000, a large sum of money in the 1850s.

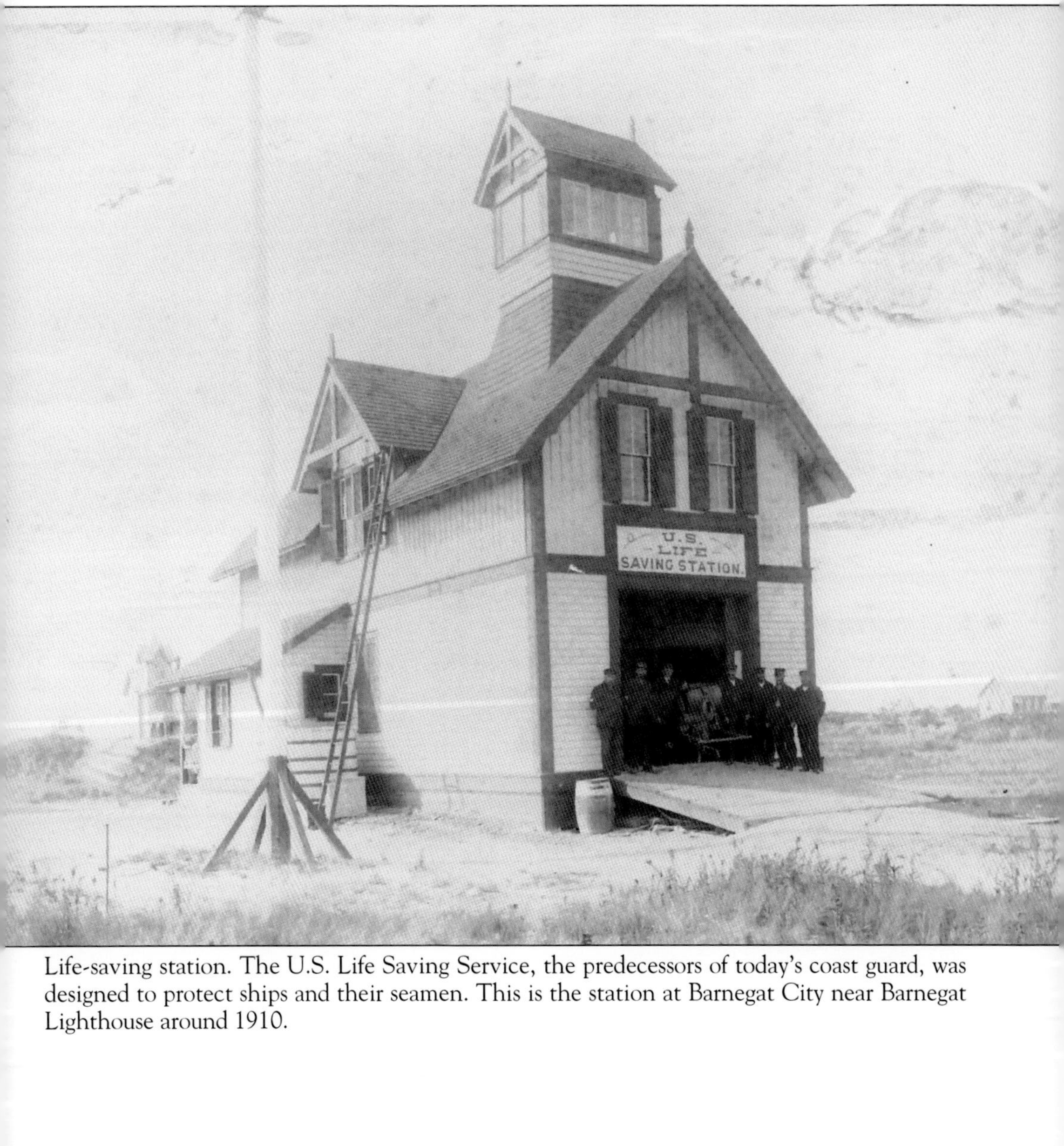

Life-saving station. The U.S. Life Saving Service, the predecessors of today's coast guard, was designed to protect ships and their seamen. This is the station at Barnegat City near Barnegat Lighthouse around 1910.

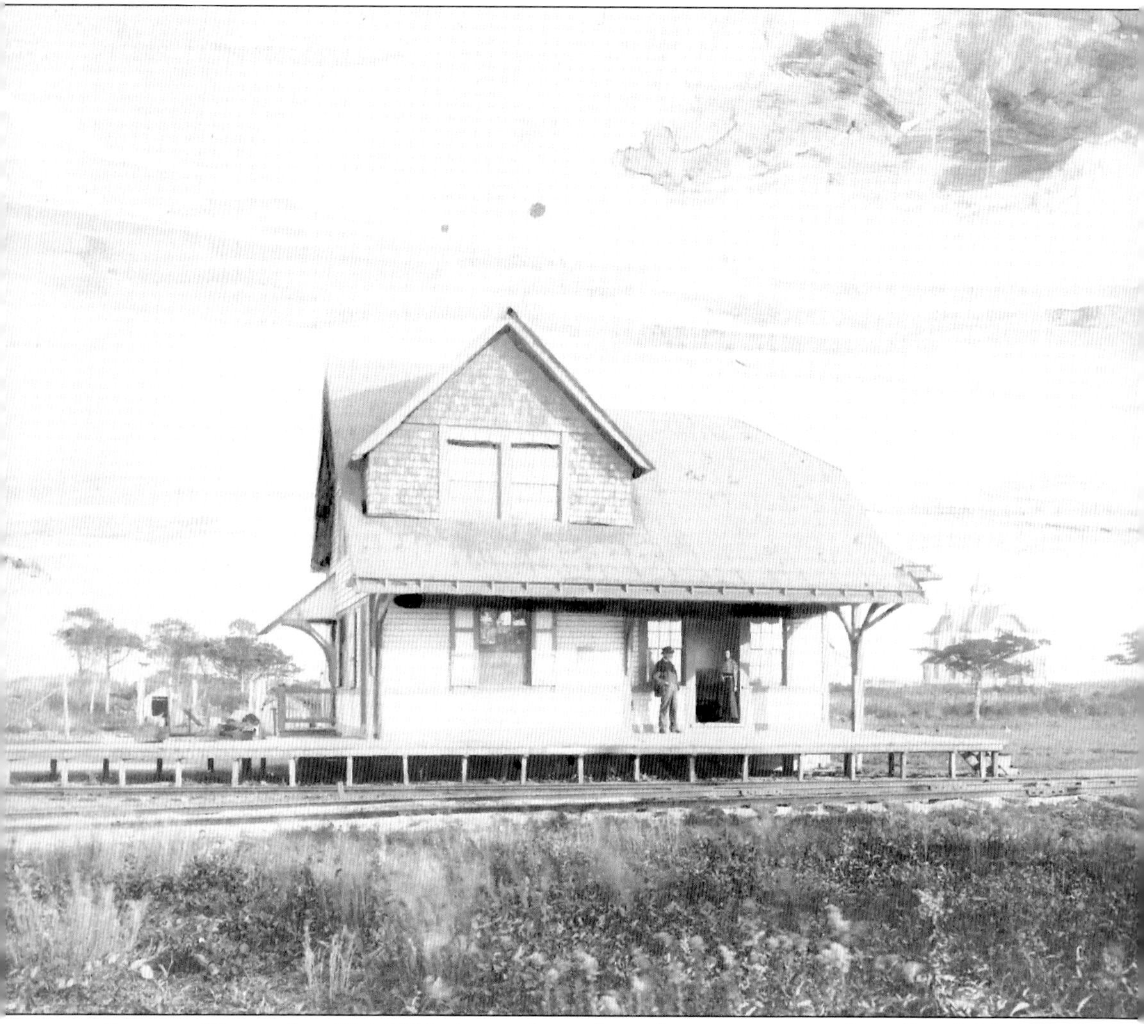

Barnegat City station. This 1911 picture shows the wide-open spaces on Long Beach Island back around the turn of the century. This station—known as the "Twelfth Street Station"—was on the railroad line from Barnegat City south to Beach Arlington (Ship Bottom).

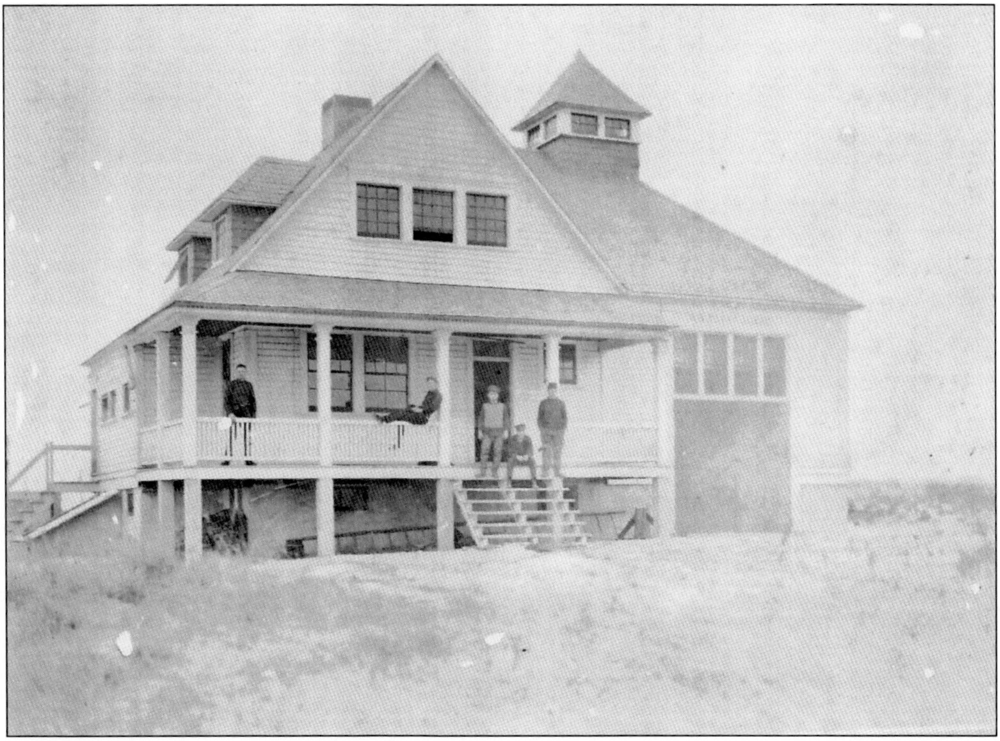

An early view of a U.S. Coast Guard station on Long Beach Island. This photograph of Bonds Station was taken around 1918. Bonds Station was located in the Holgate section of the island. The U.S. Life Saving Service merged with the Revenue Cutter Service in 1915 to form the U.S. Coast Guard.

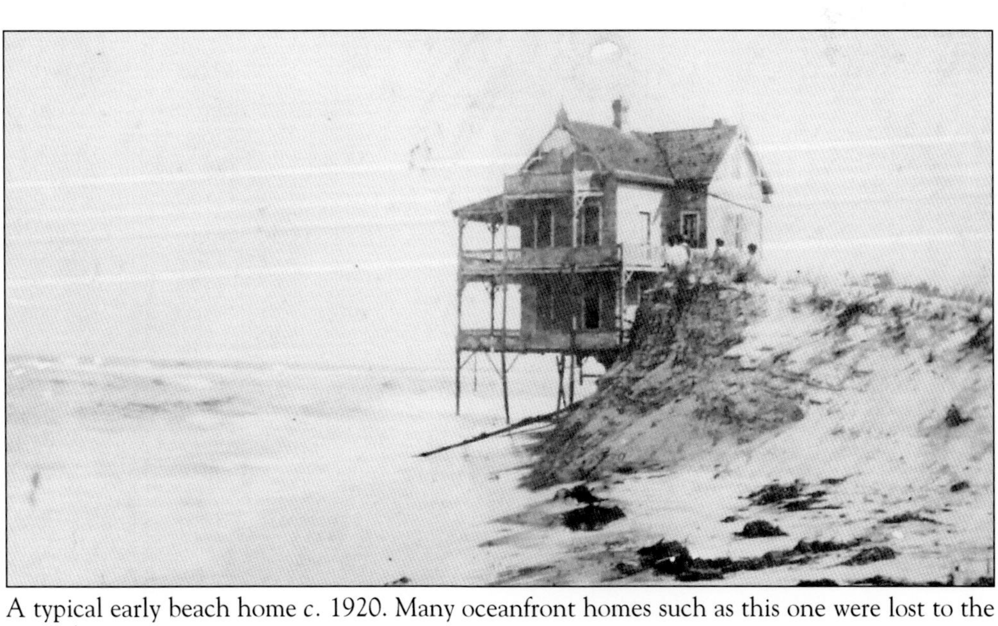

A typical early beach home c. 1920. Many oceanfront homes such as this one were lost to the sea in later years.

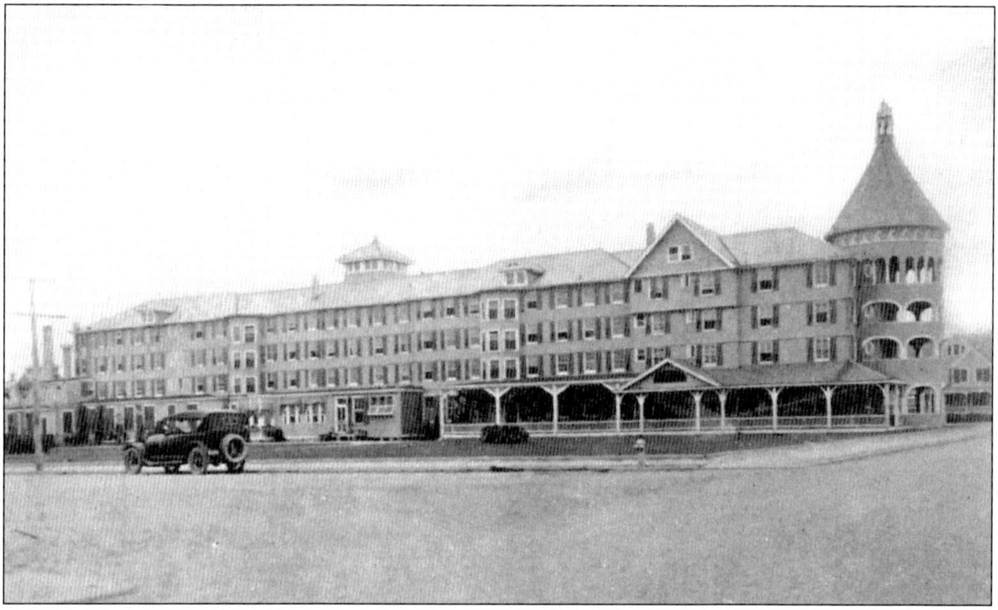

Beach Haven, known as the shining star of Long Beach Island. Here stands the Engleside Hotel around 1918. Built in 1876, it could accommodate over three hundred guests. It was one of many large hotels at the time in Beach Haven.

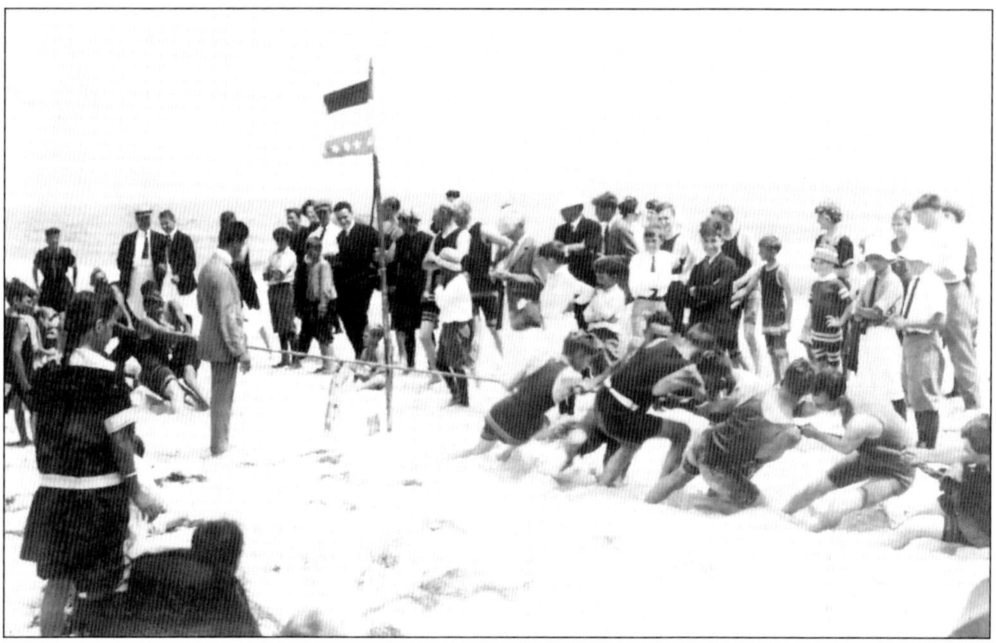

Beach Haven tug-of-war. This is a typical beach scene on Long Beach Island around 1913. Often these competitions were staged between lifeguard crews. Such activities often drew large crowds.

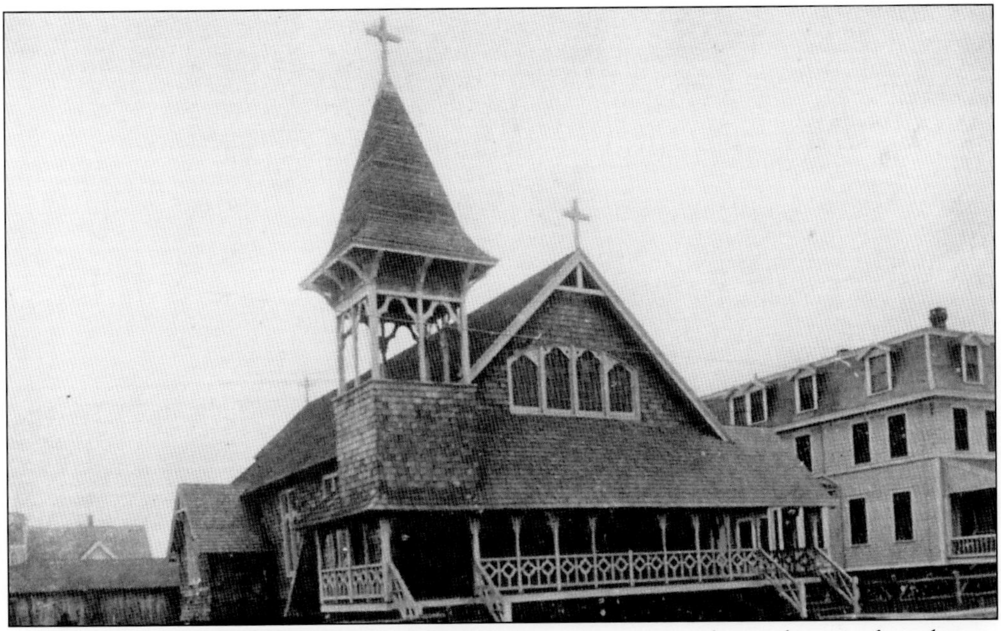

A 1908 view of the Episcopal church in Beach Haven. It was one of many houses of worship on Long Beach Island.

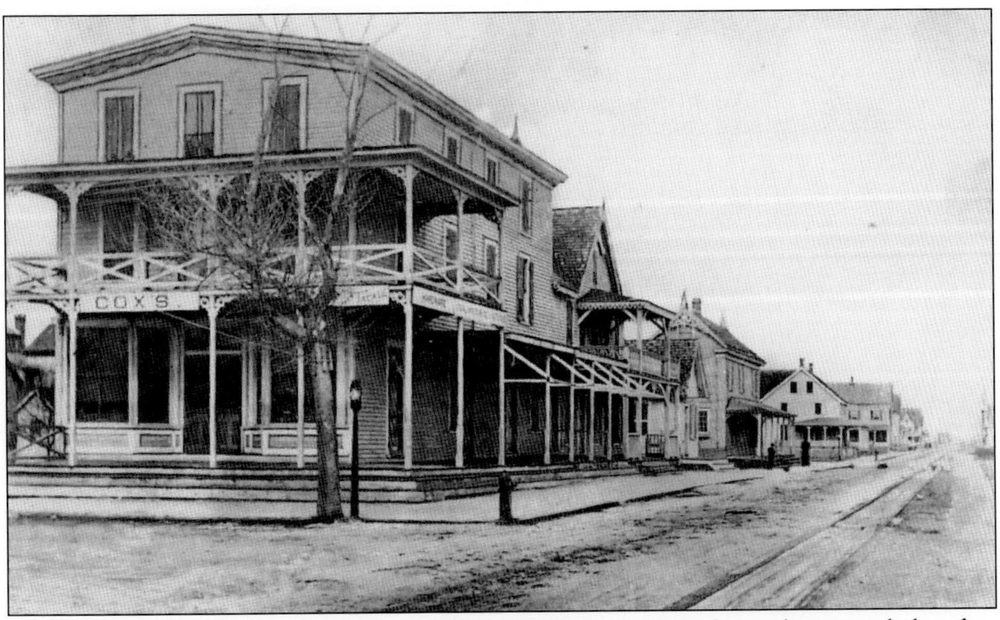

Beach Haven downtown. Beach Haven had a very concentrated population and therefore required a proper business district. Shown here is a 1911 view of Cox's Hardware, a general store, and the post office.

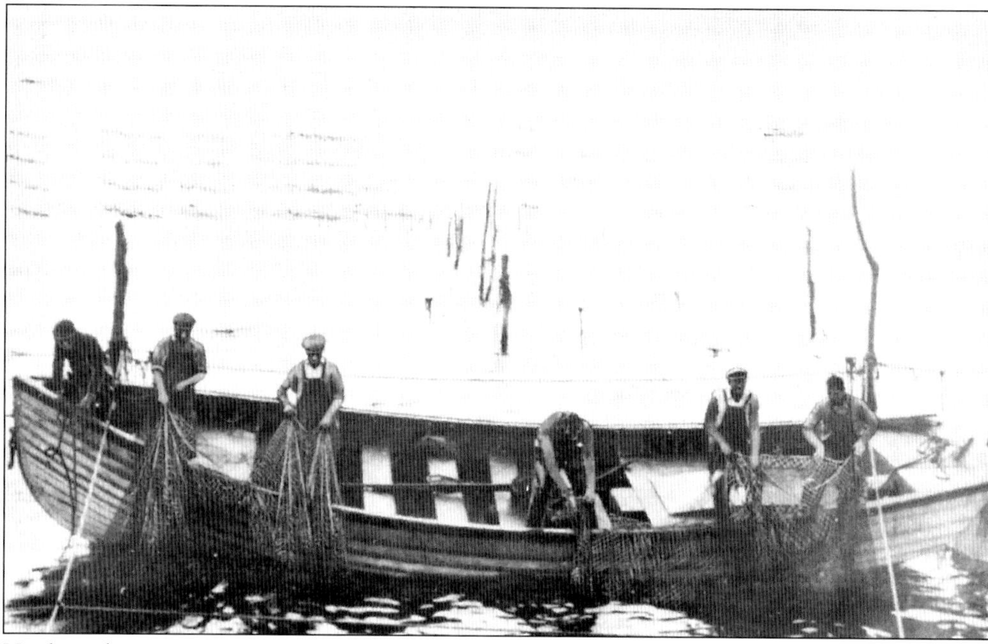

Hauling the nets at Beach Haven *c.* 1941. Fishing has always been a pastime as well as an important industry in this area.

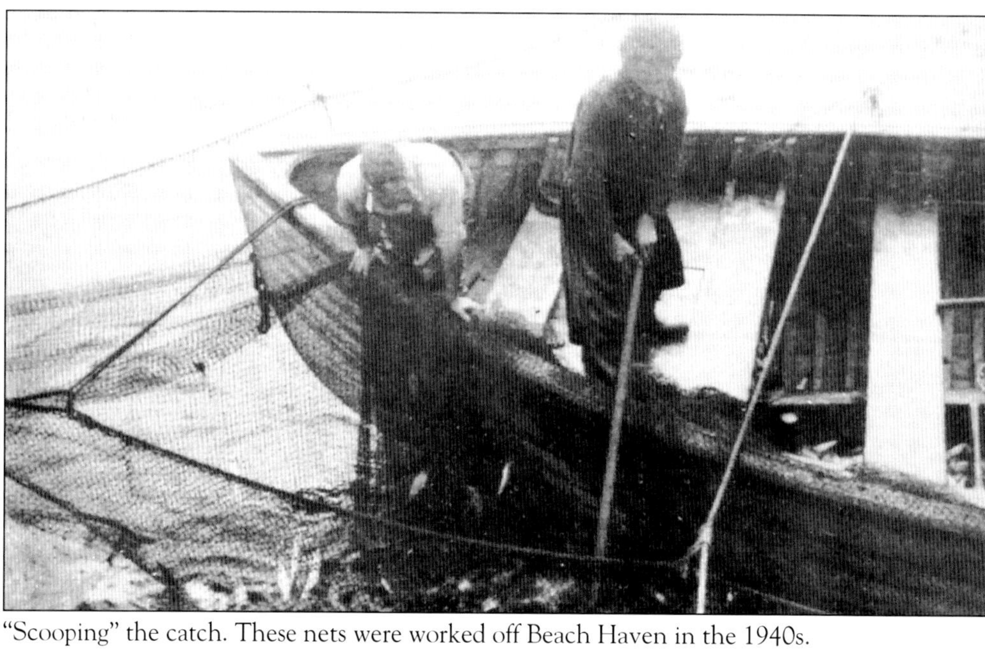

"Scooping" the catch. These nets were worked off Beach Haven in the 1940s.

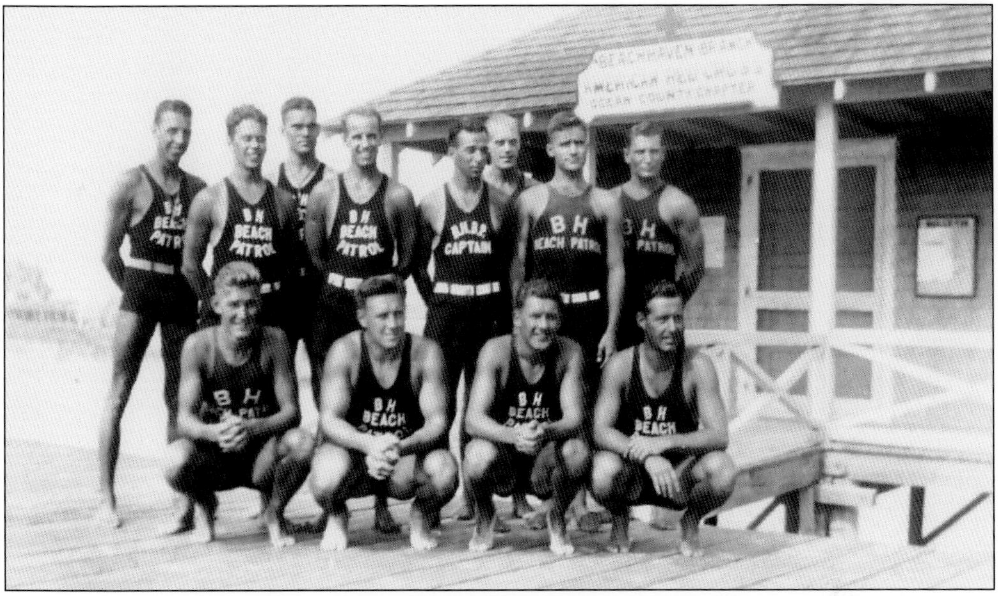

Early view of the Beach Haven Patrol of the Red Cross Life Guard. Crews such as these manned stations up and down the island at public swimming areas.

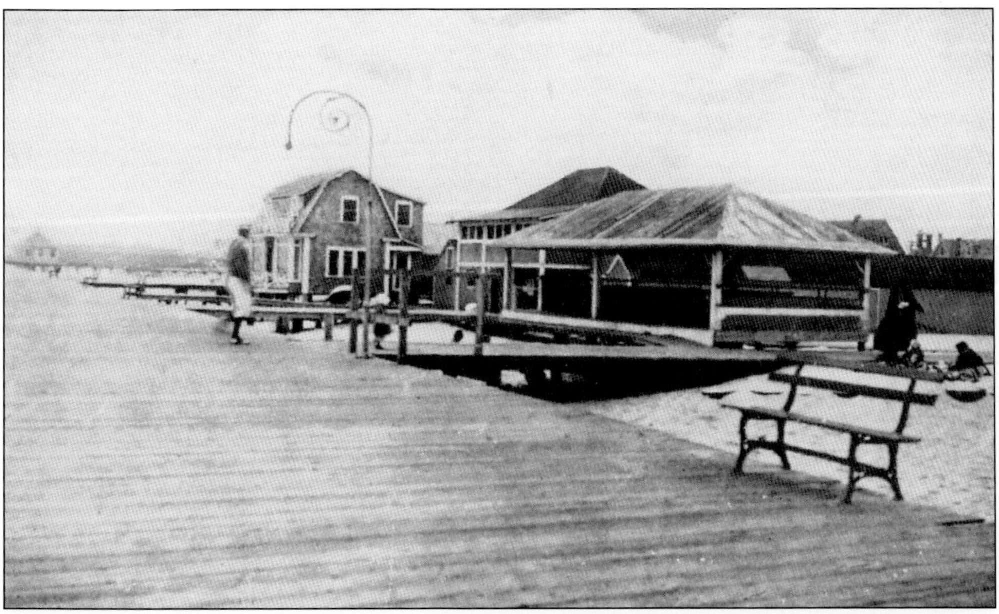

Beach Haven boardwalk. Although it was not lined with amusements, the boardwalk at Beach Haven existed as early as 1905. Shown here are the "Come and See Shop" and the Beach Haven bathhouses.

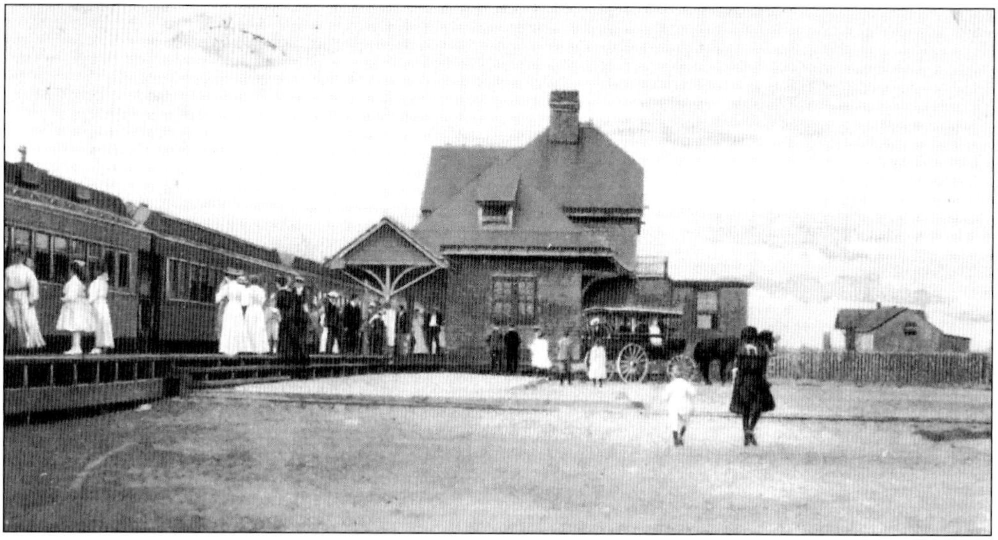

Vacation arrivals. In order to transport guests arriving at the Beach Haven station, many hotels not accessible by the street railway offered horse-drawn hacks or jitneys. This view was taken around 1908.

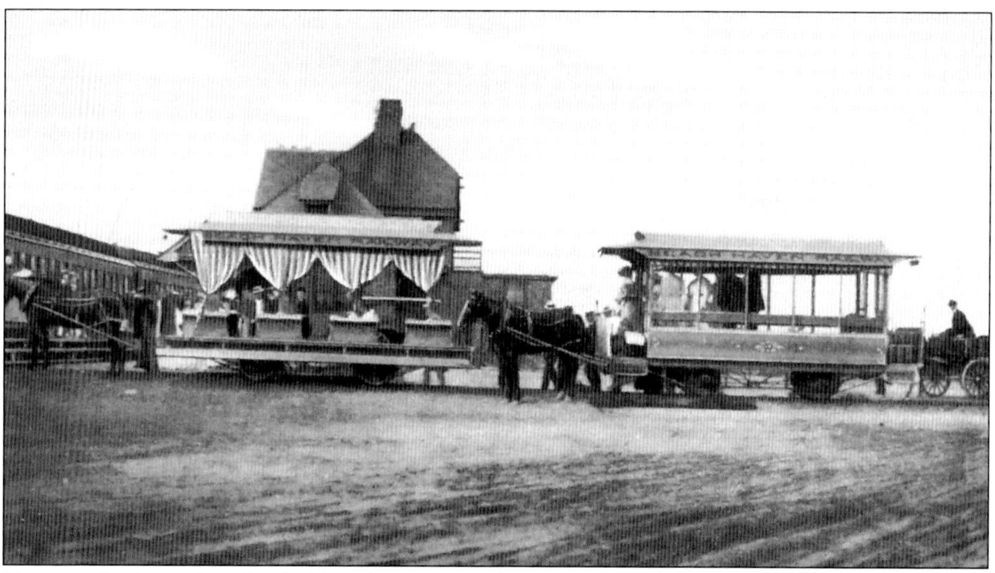

To serve the larger hotels, the Beach Haven Railroad—or "rapid transit"—was created. A series of tracks were laid from the railroad station to the hotels in 1884, and these were used by a very small steam engine. It was later replaced by horse-drawn trolleys, which continued until automobiles became commonplace.